Hill Walkers
Donegal

*38 Hill and Sea cliff Routes for the
Stroller and Mountaineer*

David Herman

SHANKSMARE PUBLICATIONS

"In the mountains you forget to count the days"
– Chinese proverb

DONEGAL

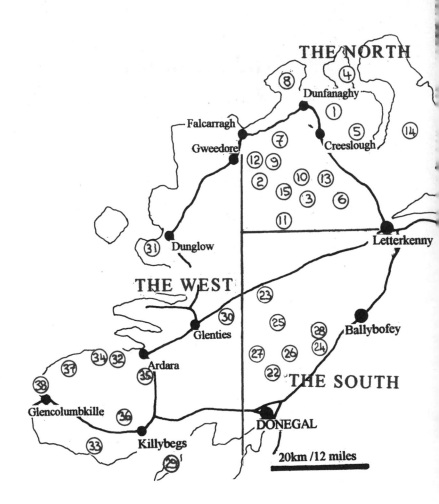

Carndonagh

Moville

INISHOWEN

Buncrana

DERRY

CONTENTS

Introduction

What's New; A Quick Look Around; How to Use this Book; Checking the Routes; Getting to Donegal; Getting Around Inside Donegal; Accommodation; Maps; Long Distance Walks; Safety; What to Carry with You; Rights of Way; A Few Route Selections; They're your Mountains Too – Get Involved!

Routes with Major Variations

WHAT'S NEW

This is the second edition of this little book, the first having been published in 1995. For the present edition the book size has been made a little more compatible with the average pocket size; the routes have been checked, mostly in the spring and autumn of 1999, some routes have been modified and others added. All this means that, even if you have the old edition you might be tempted to purchase this one. Specifically, completely new routes have been added in the Fanad Peninsula (route 14), near Glenties (route 30), along the cliffs north-east of Glencolumbkille (route 37), in the Slieve Snaght area (route 15) and the Barnesmore mountains (route 28).

Many other routes have been substantially modified from those given in the 1995 edition.

Looking at hill walking in Donegal in general, we must welcome the recent extension of Glenveagh National Park. Not only can walkers explore this beautiful area as of right but we can be sure that it will continue to be well and sensitively managed.

A QUICK LOOK AROUND

The county of Donegal is an excellent area for hill-walking, as it encompasses challenging peaks, wild and remote uplands, rocky mountain terrain and marvellous sea cliffs.

Leaving the details for later, I will describe the four main hill-walking areas in broad outline, each of these areas corresponding to a section in the book and each described in more detail in the introduction to each section.

The **North** is dominated by three bare, rocky lines of mountains, called collectively the Highlands. Of these three, the northern is graced by probably the most easily recognised mountain in Ireland, Errigal (752m) and the middle by Slieve Snaght (683m). Some of this area is in Glenveagh National Park. North of the Highlands are rugged peninsulas offering good coastal walking.

East of the Highlands is the large peninsula of **Inishowen**, in which the characteristic orientation of the Highlands is faintly continued. Here there is a tiny rocky line of mountains and, in the centre of the peninsula, bulky but unimpressive rolling uplands rising to 615m. There is also plenty of good coastal walking.

The principal mountains of the **South** are a small knot of undulating uplands, the Blue Stacks, which rise to 674m. The central Blue Stacks is a fascinating area of bare rocky knolls, while the rest is grassy and more mundane. As well as the Blue Stacks proper, the hills in the immediate area are included in this section.

Lastly, the **West**, that is the western coastal strip and the bulge of peninsula in the south-west sometimes called Rossaun. It hardly needs to be said that this is an excellent area for cliff-top walks, of which the best-known, though not the best, is that at Slieve League (595m). Inland, there are good walking areas, though you need to be a little discriminating, as the uplands in places degenerate into bleak moorland.

HOW TO USE THIS BOOK

I have tried to cover all the best and most characteristic of the mountain areas in the county. In doing so, I have taken a 'light-and-shade' approach, that is I do not describe everywhere and every route as being superlatively good. All routes have some favourable characteristics but some are better than others - in my opinion. Your verdict might well be quite different.

The Maps The extracts from the full colour 1:50 000 Ordnance Survey (OS) maps that accompany nearly all the route descriptions will get you round the route (assuming you do not stray too far!) but they are emphatically not as useful as the originals from which they are taken. *The map extracts do not necessarily cover route variations.* Remember that the side of each square on the map represents 1km and that if converting from grid to compass bearing to add 9°. The extracts are supplemented in red by the line of the route; by symbols indicating features that are missing from the original maps eg cliffs and by landmarks, some of which are small, that are useful as reassurance points or important for navigation. These landmarks are emphasised in red in the text. All symbols are explained on the inside back cover.

I have not indicated sea cliffs on the map extracts: if I had indicated them, the symbols would have obscured interesting coastal detail.

The Walking Time given with each route description and the intermediate walking time given at important points on the routes are just that; they do not allow time for rests, photographs or consulting the map. They are based on a walking speed of 4km/hr on the flat and a climbing rate of 500m/hr, so for instance it should take $1^1/_2$ hrs to walk 4km with a climb of 250m. This is not a superhuman rate; it reflects mountain terrain where there are few paths and tracks, the situation that pertains over most of Donegal and indeed Ireland. Where the terrain justifies it this walking time is adjusted for difficult terrain (eg steep *descents*, rough vegetation) or easy terrain (eg tracks).

Metric versus Imperial I have used metric wherever feasible - if you simply can't think metric use the scale on the inside back cover. Imperial units are used when giving distances by car, as they are usually equipped with milometers.

Grid References These are the four or six digit numbers, preceded by the letters 'GR' which appear in this book after some locations, particularly the start of walks. The figure uniquely identifies the location on most maps. The system is explained on all OS maps.

CHECKING THE ROUTES

Most of the routes were completely walked in 1999 or early 2000. The exceptions are a few of the shorter routes (3, 6, 29) which are mostly on track and road, and a few longer routes which were only partly walked (19, 31, 25, 35) or only whose beginning and end were checked (4, 9, 17, 18).

The major change from 1994, when the routes were first checked, is the increase in fencing. I am glad to report that all landowners I encountered were friendly and helpful, just as they were then.

GETTING TO DONEGAL

By Sea and Air

The nearest ferry ports are at Larne and Belfast, with Dublin/Dun Laoire farther away. There is an airport with regular flights from Dublin and Glasgow at Kincasslagh near Dunglow (☎ 075-48284). Other airports are at Derry, Knock, Belfast and Dublin, working roughly from nearest to farthest.

By Car

The main roads into the county are shown on any small-scale road map and it is pointless to laboriously duplicate the information here. In general access is easier from Northern Ireland than from the Republic: there is a motorway (the M1) from Belfast to a little less than half-way to Donegal town. The main roads from the Republic (the N2/A5 from Dublin to North Donegal, the N3/A46 from Dublin to South Donegal and the N15 from Sligo), though of fairly good standard, are far from being motorways.

By Public Transport

There is a frequent Ulsterbus service from Belfast to Derry directly (routes 211 and 212) and to Derry via Strabane (route 273). From Derry there are local services to many towns and villages in north Donegal (See 'Getting Around Inside Donegal' below.)

The main Bus Eireann (☎ 074-21309) express bus services into Donegal are the table 30 (from Dublin to Donegal town via Cavan, about $4^{1}/_{4}$ hours), table 32 (Dublin to Letterkenny via Monaghan, about 4 hours), table 64 (Galway to Donegal town and Letterkenny, about 5 hrs) and table 69 (Westport through Sligo to Derry, about $6^{1}/_{2}$ hours). The 64 service runs between the two best local bus termini in the county, Donegal town and Letterkenny. Details of all BE services (express and local) are given in their timetable.

McGeehan's Coaches (☎ 075-46101) run a daily service to and from Dublin, with two routes serving towns in south Donegal, terminating in Glencolumbkille and Dunglow. McGinley's Coaches (☎ 074-35201) run a daily service to and from Dublin, terminating in Annagary (GR 7919), and on the way serving numerous towns and villages in north Donegal. North-West Busways (☎ 077-82619) has services from Dublin to Inishowen.

There is no rail service into Donegal. The nearest stations are at Sligo to the south and Derry to the east.

GETTING AROUND INSIDE DONEGAL

Getting Around by Car

The national secondary road that you will get most familiar with in Donegal is the N56, which follows a circuitous route roughly following the coast from Letterkenny in the north-east to Donegal town in the south. It is of variable quality and the signposting is adequate.

Regional (R-designated) roads are of course not so good and some of the minor roads (unclassified) are almost more pothole than tarmac. The watchword must therefore be: take it easy or you will take it to the garage.

Many minor roads leading to the starting points of walks in this book have no signposting or what is worse, signposting that you cannot rely on. This arises because many finger signposts (ie the ones which are retained on their posts only at one end) are all too frequently either turned to an incorrect position or pointing ambiguously between two roads. It's a nuisance to have to keep one finger glued to the map or half an eye on the milometer but this is preferable to the annoyance caused by getting lost before you even start the walk.

Ailt an Chorráin	Burtonport
An Charraig	Carrick
An Clochán Liath	Dunglow
An Dúchoraidh	Doocharry
Ard an Rátha	Ardara
Cill Charthaigh	Kilcar
Croithlí	Crolly
Gaoth Dobhair	Gweedore
Cleann Cholm Cille	Glencolumbkille
Leitir Ceanainn	Letterkenny
Na Cealla Beaga	Killybegs

There is another hazard in signposting in or near Irish-speaking areas (or more accurately, supposedly Irish-speaking areas). This is that, in magnificent defiance of all logic and reason, the signposting is entirely in Irish, though the towns indicated are known to all and sundry by their English versions. In the accompanying panel the Irish version of towns that you are likely to encounter on signposts in Irish only and which differ significantly from the English version are given.

Getting Around by Local Bus Service
Several bus companies operate within Donegal.

Bus Eireann (☎ 074-21309) has services in most of the county except the north. The services of most use to walkers are:
* Table 480 between Donegal town and Ballybofey.
* Table 490 between Killybegs, Glencolumbkille and Malinmore (a few kilometres to its west).
* Table 492 between Killybegs, Glenties and Portnoo (marginal use).
* Table 494 between Donegal town and Killybegs.

North-West Busways (☎ 077-82619) serves Inishowen. *The Swilly Bus Service* (☎ 074-22863) serves the Gweedore area and the villages on the N56 facing the north coast. It also provides services in Inishowen and to the Fanad Peninsula directly to its west.

O'Donnell Coaches (☎ 075-48114) and *McGinley Coaches* (☎ 074-35201) also serve the Gweedore area and the villages on the N56 facing the north coast. O'Donnell's also runs a service from Annagary, near Dunglow, to Killybegs. *McGeehan Coaches* (☎ 075-46150) serve the west and south-west of the county.

All these services give the impression that the whole county is well served with buses. Unfortunately this isn't true, as most of the services are infrequent, so that you must check the current timetable carefully. Note also that all services have a minimum fare, which may make a short journey uneconomical.

All local buses will stop and pick up anywhere as long as it is safe to do so. Services are generally better on weekdays than on Saturdays and especially Sundays.

All relevant services are noted under the appropriate route.

Other Means of Transport

You can hire a taxi or minibus in most of the towns and if you are a large group this may turn out to be cheaper and more flexible than bus. Details may be obtained by enquiring locally or in the yellow pages of the phone book. And don't forget the humble bike, which may by hired in several towns and villages.

Hitch-hiking

This is an acceptable form of getting around in rural Ireland and it is usually not difficult to get a lift, though if you are soaked to the skin, dripping wet and carrying a large equally wet rucksack your chances will not be enhanced. This is usually the time when you really want a lift! Women travelling alone after dark might be advised to avoid hitching.

ACCOMMODATION

A wide variety of holiday accommodation is available especially along the coast and in the larger towns. Hotel, guest houses and self-catering accommodation is widespread in the county. Details of all these types of accommodation are given in the relevant Bord Failte brochures or in local newspapers.

If you are specifically on a walking holiday, among the locations you might consider are the string of small towns along the N56 from **Creeslough** to **Gortahork** (these towns are suitable for the mountains of the North); **Buncrana** for Inishowen; **Letterkenny** (not too far from good walking areas and a hub for the Swilly Bus service); **Dunglow**, **Ardara** or **Glenties** for the West and **Glencolumbkille** or **Killybegs** for Rossaun. **Donegal town**, a good bus centre, is the well placed for the Blue Stacks and some of the mountains to the west eg Slieve League.

There are adventure centres at Gartan Lough in the north and at Malinmore near Glencolumbkille which offer accommodation.

More spartan types might prefer youth hostels or independent hostels.

There are youth hostels at Tra na Rosann on the north coast, at Errigal convenient to the best of the Highland area and at Crohy Head, both on the remote west coast and at Ball Hill near Donegal town. Note that though there are always self-catering facilities in hostels few will serve meals that are not booked in advance. Details from An Oige (☎ 01-830 4555).

The Independent Hostel group has hostels in Donegal town, Letterkenny, Dunkineely, Dunlewy, Kilcar, Glencolumbkille, Carrowkeel, Ardara, Ballybofey, Crolly, Malin Head, and Dunglow. Details from ☎ 073-30130 or http://www.eroicapub.com/ihi.

MAPS

The mapping of the entire county is excellent and is covered on a series of layer-tinted maps, on a scale of 1:50 000 with a contour interval of 10m; the north on sheets 1-3, the centre on sheet 6 and the south on sheets 10 and 11.

Since these are the maps you will most probably use it is worth while pointing out a few of their more important characteristics.

- Cliffs are not explicitly depicted. In the case of some sections of sea cliff, the contour lines have been omitted altogether.
- What are shown on the map as forest tracks may in fact be firebreaks. Tracks take account of the lie of the land; firebreaks run up hill and down dale regardless of the slope.
- The thin black or grey lines shown in some upland areas are field boundaries of some kind, usually walls or earthbanks.
- Few paths and no footbridges are shown.
- Streams in uplands are badly depicted, with many fordable ones shown by intimidatingly thick lines.
- It is often difficult to deduce from the map exactly where waterfalls are.
- Inexplicably, especially in the older editions, there may not be a trig pillar on the ground where one is indicated on the map, and there may be one where one is not indicated. Discrepancies are noted in the text.

The alternative to the 1:50 000 series is the old 1:126 720 series, now no longer being printed, though it is not hard to pick up copies. The whole county is covered on sheets 1 and 3. These maps have a contour interval of 100ft and show cliffs explicitly but not over-accurately. They might be a useful assurance if you are using the 1:50 000 extracts given here and are afraid you might wander off the limited area they cover. They are also good for identifying faraway features.

If you are in Glenveagh National Park, ask for the *old* National Park leaflet as it contains a map that covers the Park area around the Centre and Lough Beagh. Its scale is 1:63 360 and the contour interval is 100ft. It shows cliffs explicitly and quite accurately, the only map to do so.

There is more about suitable maps in each route description.

LONG DISTANCE WALKS

Five long distance walks are to be launched in Donegal in 2000. Four are collectively called Bealach na Gaeltachta; each of them runs through designated Irish-speaking areas. Each walk is approximately 50-70km long and is looped. All the routes traverse remote country in the west of the county. The other route is the Blue Stack Way, is 120km long and will join up with Bealach na Gaeltachta. Details from Donegal county council (☎ 074-72222).

SAFETY

Walkers unused to Irish conditions will be excused if they are asked to read carefully a section on safety, given that they have noted that the highest mountain in the entire county is a puny 750m high.

Do not be misled by such seemingly insignificant heights! Irish mountains in general (and Donegal is no exception) are wild, remote and worthy of respect. It is noteworthy that a high proportion of the fatal accidents in recent years has been suffered by visitors, who did not realise the conditions they were to face.

But let's not be too timid. If you take reasonable precautions and do not try walking in conditions for which you are unprepared, you will enjoy your time in the mountains and return to base safely and with a sense of having achieved something worthwhile.

So, what are 'reasonable precautions'?

- You will get some idea of what to expect on each route from the section on 'Difficulties'. Of course, conditions vary greatly depending on the weather, but you can assume that unless the route is entirely or almost entirely on road, track or path you should wear walking boots.

- This section will also give you an idea of how hard it will be to find your way round the route, but remember that the easiest route to follow in bad visibility may be harder than the hardest in good. Cloud and fog make all the difference to navigation. As well as the obvious lack of visibility they are disorienting and distorting, so that what is in reality a minor hill near at hand will appear through cloud like a major mountain much further away.

- It is advisable not to walk alone and better to have at least three persons, thus allowing one to stay with the injured after an accident and one to try to get help. You can call the mountain rescue services by phoning 999 or 112.

- Leave word at base of where you intend to go and when you should be back.

WHAT TO CARRY WITH YOU

If you were to carry all the safety equipment that some experts tell you to carry, you would be so weighed down that you wouldn't be able to walk.

The most important item to get right are boots, as mentioned in the section 'Safety' above. Apart from that there are only a few things that you really must carry. These include food and a flask with a hot liquid, a whistle and a map and compass. Unless the day looks uncommonly settled and likely to remain so, you should take a waterproof. Lastly, you need a rucksack to put everything else in. Anything else is optional or depends mainly on the weather and the route.

RIGHTS OF WAY

Nearly all the land over which you walk in Donegal, the major exception being Glenveagh National Park, belongs to someone and you are his or her uninvited guest. Landowners generally will not object to your walking across their land but do not abuse the privilege - *and that is what it is*. Please behave accordingly. Specifically:

- Park carefully. Remember that farm machinery, which may be as wide as the road you are parked on, may have to pass.

- Respect the privacy of the occupants of houses. If you have to walk through a farmyard, ask permission and do so quietly.

- Do not take dogs into sheep-rearing country, that is nearly everywhere in the mountains.
- Do not stand on fence wire. It may look the same afterwards but will have been irreparably damaged. Find a place where you can cross without damaging the wire – after all farmers have to do this also.
- Leave gates, open or closed, as you found them and if you have to climb them do so at the hinged side.
- Do not litter in the mountains - or anywhere else for that matter.
- Exchange a few words with farmers you encounter; do not pass by in surly silence.

A FEW ROUTE SELECTIONS

The following selection of routes in all parts of the county does not cover simply the best routes as this would not give sufficiently varied terrain. They may be worth considering if you have a limited time in Donegal:
- Routes 12 (Errigal) or 10 (Slieve Snaght) in the North, two imposing mountains giving wide and spectacular panoramas.
- Route 19 (the Urris Hills) in Inishowen, a narrow, rocky ridge.
- Route 26 (Circuit of Lough Belshade) in the Blue Stacks, a memorable circuit in rocky, austere terrain.
- Route 37 (Glenlough), the best of the marvellous sea-cliff scenery this area has to offer.

THEY'RE YOUR MOUNTAINS TOO – GET INVOLVED!

I've said this so many times but I still feel it is worth repeating: I wish that we, the Irish people, showed as much care for the environment as our beautiful country deserves. But we don't. Certainly, we are strong on legislation, but it is a completely different matter when it comes to implementing it. Poor enforcement combined with a 'couldn't care less' attitude on the part of too many people have left littering and dumping in towns and the countryside. In the course of researching this book I have come across more than a few instances of such carelessness, and if I have forborne to mention them it is not because I was not both saddened and angry.

Under these circumstances I can only suggest that you get involved in an organisation that cares about the environment and that if you are in a walking club that you make sure that there is an environment group and get involved in it.

The core mountain area of North Donegal is the Highlands, the sternest and wildest area of the whole county. It consists of three long narrow ranges, all of which run roughly south-west to north-east. The straightline layout of all three ranges makes looped walks a little difficult but not impossible to devise, so local buses may be useful for A to B routes.

The northern range, though only about 12km long, contains the very different peaks of Errigal and Muckish, two of the best-known mountains in Ireland. Errigal, a scree-sided cone rising to a tiny summit at 751m is the highest mountain in the county (routes 7, 9, 12), and contrasts greatly with Muckish (666m), which has an extensive summit plateau. Between these two are the three elegant peaks of the Aghlas (603m), which form an excellent walking area with Errigal, but are separated from Muckish by a large area of soggy ground.

Southwards is a longer range, the central part of which is an area of bare granite rock with characteristic steep-sided grikes across it. The range rises to Slieve Snaght (678m), which is surrounded by great walking country. The two ends of this range are wetter and less interesting, though it is still possible to get challenging walks around Glentornan Lough and Dooish (652m) (routes 10, 11, 13), the highest point in Glenveagh National Park (route 3).

The most southerly of these three ranges is the lower Glendowan Mountains, most of which is in the National Park. This is a remote and less exciting area, with the area to the south of Lough Beagh being exceptionally wet and soggy.

Even in the mountain areas, unencumbered as they are by extensive forestry, easier walks are to be found (routes 2-4, 6), mostly near lakes. These walks are all on tracks or remote roads and give excellent views of the higher peaks.

North of the mountain area is a highly indented, rocky, partly cliff-bound coast facing the Atlantic and offering excellent coastal walks (routes 1, 5, 8), though this coast hasn't the remote ambience of the inland areas to the south.

Separated from the main mountain area are the hills around Lough Salt (route 5) and the long, narrow Knockalla Ridge (route 14). These isolated mountain areas offer easier walks in not very remote surrounds.

Maps 1, 2, 6. ■

ROUTE 1: ARDS FOREST PARK

Situated between Dunfanaghy (4 miles) and Creeslough (2 miles) on the N56, Ards Forest Park has a great variety of scenery and terrain: fenland, lakes, beaches, dunes, rocky faces, deciduous and coniferous trees. It also has a wealth of cultural remains: a dolmen, ring forts. There is a map in the carpark that gives details of the various nature trails and other features. You should easily get a walk of up to 8km or so on the tracks and paths in the park. A small fee is payable at the entrance. **Buses** Swilly Bus, McGinley's or O'Donnell's. ■

ROUTE 2: DUNLEWY LOUGH

This gives an easy and scenic stroll along the side of a valley and through a pleasant wood. Marvellous mountain views though curiously little close viewing of the lake circled. If you don't like walking on roads, no matter how scenic, it might be as well to make it a there-and-back walk to the point indicated below.

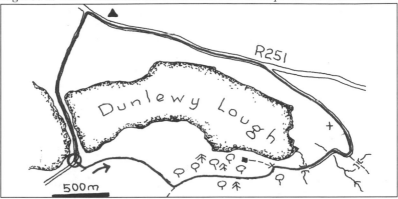

Getting There You can start at any point on the R251, which forms much of the circuit. Let's say that you start on the south side of the causeway separating Dunlewy Lough from Lough Nacung Upper (GR 905192). It is reached by passing the youth hostel at Dunlewy on the right, taking the next left, crossing the causeway and parking immediately on waste ground.

Walking Time 2 hours (distance 8km, climb 90m) but you will probably want to take it at a much more leisurely pace than Naismith allows.

Difficulties Some rough and sometimes wet ground to start.

Map None necessary.

Route Walk south-east over rough ground for a few metres with a forest plantation on the right and then turn left onto a track. Keep on this track to make an undulating progress over open ground and, at a tee where a vague track heads right into open country, turn left with the main track into a wood. At the nearby tee turn right and continue straight ahead on the main track to another tee, where there are imposing gate pillars off to the left. Turn right at this tee to emerge from the wood onto a road with a pleasant stream on the right and a derelict church farther up to the left (0.75 hours). A good place to rest and from which to return by the same route if you don't fancy a road walk. If you want to go on, take the hairpin bend to pass the church and continue upward to the R251. Turn left here and of course left again beyond the youth hostel.

Poisoned Glen Variation While you are in the area it is well worth making the effort to see the Poisoned Glen, surely one of the most memorable easily accessible mountain areas in Ireland. There is more about the Glen under route 10.

Take the track at the hairpin bend just before the derelict church. It leads across a bridge and beyond it follow the stream on the right into the Glen. The end of the Glen is about 2.5km away (about 0.75 hours each way). ■

ROUTE 3: GLENVEAGH

An A to B walk, all on track or path, to the Castle which forms the centre point of the National Park, along a straight valley flanked by high hills. Maybe a little too much sameness for those who demand the spice of life.

Getting There Let's say you are in your car at the well signposted entrance to the National Park (GR 0323). To drive to the start of the route, turn right out of the Park, follow the signs for Church Hill for about 6 miles to cross the Leannan River (signed). Keep on the main road immediately after the bridge, but then turn next right off it to reach Glendowan. Continue straight ahead for a further 4 miles to a right-angle bend to the left, parking here on waste ground on the right (about 14 miles in all). You can also reach this point on the R254 from Doocharry, about 9 miles away.

The walk ends at the National Park's Visitor Centre, to which the non-walking driver should return.

Walking Time 1.75 hours (distance 8km, no significant climb).

Difficulties None.

Map None necessary.

Route Cross the gate at the waste ground and take the track beyond. Keep walking straight ahead! The Castle and Lough Beagh soon come into view in the distance beyond a long, straight, narrow, glacial valley flanked by steep sides over which pours the occasional spectacular waterfall. The track eventually reaches the shores of Lough Beagh, whose beauty is once again revealed now that rhododendron have been cleared. At the Castle pick up the bus that will take you to the Visitor Centre, where the non-walking driver will have paid the appropriate fee for you into the National Park.

There-and-Back Variation From the Castle (GR 0220) walk around the outbuildings to take the track south-west along the shores of Lough Beagh. Just beyond the lake take what is at first a good track on the left sloping sharply upward. It deteriorates as it climbs and peters out in a high, narrow valley with exceedingly wet ground underfoot. Return by the same route when the ground gets too aqueous (that is, at about the point where it nearly levels).

Walking time is about 2.5 hours in all but of course it does depend on exactly where you turn back. ■

ROUTE 4: MELMORE HEAD

Lovely coastal scenery, especially on its western side, with good, ever-changing views. The terrain changes rapidly from secluded sandy beaches and grassy slopes to low but impressive sea-cliffs and expanses of rock plunging into the sea.

Getting There In Carrigart (GR 1336), which is 4.5 miles away, take the R248 (signed). After 1.0 miles fork gently right and continue straight ahead to pass a viewpoint on the right after another 2.6 miles. Turn next right, and left at the bottom of the hill to park in Tranarossan carpark (GR 119419). **Bus** Try Gallagher's (☎ 074-37037). **Walking Time** 3 hours (distance 10km, climb about 220m).

Difficulties None, though you should give yourself plenty of time for negotiating fences (which should be safeguarded) and slippery, treacherous rock

Map No map necessary, but take sheet 2 if you have it.

Route You hardly need any guide to this area. Walk to and along Tranarossan Beach, climb directly north-east to pt 163m, whose shoulder rises directly from the beach. At the top you will see the whole route and a lot more besides, with Horn Head and Tory Island prominent to the west.

Descend to Boyeeghter Beach (which is not suitable for swimming because of its strong undercurrents) and

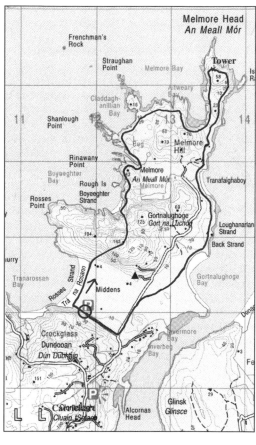

after that simply continue along the coast to the promontory of Melmore Head, marked by the ruins of a tower (1.75 hours). On the return follow the track and road past several caravan parks to the start. Alternatively, and preferably, keep to the low rocky coast, here punctuated by several sandy beaches, on a longer but more scenic route. At Gortnalughoge Bay take any route to the start. ■

ROUTE 5: LOUGH SALT

Though far from the main mountain centres and surrounded by none too interesting moorland, the tiny upland area centred on Loughsalt Mountain (469m) offers easy walking with excellent wide views.

Getting There From the north, fork left (signposted) at the shrine in the village of Glen (GR 1130) and continue for $3^1/_2$ miles to the carpark on the right close to Lough Salt (GR 1226). From the south take the N56 north from Kilmacrenan, fork right shortly (signposted), ignore the turn on the right immediately after, fork left after a few hundred metres and continue straight ahead to the carpark (4 miles in all).

Buses See below.

Walking Time 2.5 hours (distance 7km, climb 360m).

Difficulties Some high vegetation after Loughsalt Mountain but otherwise fairly good underfoot and easy navigation. Don't be tempted to walk along the seemingly inviting eastern shore of Lough Salt. It's a nightmare of bad vegetation and steep slopes (mostly simultaneously).

Map Sheet 2.

Route From the carpark walk south along the road (ie with the lake on the left). Just past its end, pass a pumping station on the left, and immediately beyond it cross two stiles on that side. Incidentally, a meteor struck the western side of the mountain in 1821, and for years after the track of scorched heather ending in the lake indicated its route down the hillside. From here on, keeping clear of scree (and meteors), climb all the way north-east to the three peaks (pts 454m, 469m, about 460m) collectively called Loughsalt Mountain which lie within a few hundred metres of one another and are climbed west to east. The main peak (469m, 1 hour) is obvious from its trig pillar, set amid shattered rocks.

The rest of the route is not over-exciting. From the main peak continue to the east peak and then cross heathery country to reach the northern side of Lough Reelan. Don't descend to the lakeshore; if you keep about 50m above it you will pick up a useful path heading west. This path will take you down through turf cuttings from where a track leads to the road. Walk straight ahead for the start.

Bus Variation This route or a longer variation might be just about worth doing using the Swilly Bus, O'Donnell's, or McGinley's to Termon (GR 1122), 4km away. Take the track beside the church, turn right at the tee and next left. After that it's straight ahead.

Other Variations The main route is really too short for a full-day walk. Aided by the map you can lengthen it, though it has to be admitted that there is little out of the mundane in the area around. One route is to continue from Loughsalt

Mountain into rolling wet country to the north-east and then head west to reach the north-south tarmaced road between Glen and Lough Salt. Another is to walk tracks through remote country on the western side of Lough Greenan and over Crockmore (GR 1025).

ROUTE 6: GARTAN LOUGH

A low-level, varied route with practically no climbing, all on track or road around the wooded shores of Gartan Lough. The second half of the walk is mostly by road and might be foregone if time is pressing and a lift is available.

Getting There Start in the carpark at Glebe Gallery (1), just off the R251 (GR 0617). If a kind non-walking driver is available you can arrange to be picked up at Glendowan and so forego the second part of the walk, which is on road. To drive to Glenowen turn right out of the carpark, go straight ahead to cross the bridge over the River Leannan (signed), keep on the main road (R251) immediately beyond it and turn next right to leave it (signed Colmcille Centre). Drive straight ahead for over 3 miles to the telephone kiosk on the right (at GR 0213).

Walking Time 3.25 hours (distance 13km, climb 100m), but if you are picked up at Glendowan this time is roughly halved.

Difficulties Some wet patches, otherwise easy underfoot.

Map Sheet 6 or the *old* National Park one-inch map, but none really necessary.

Route Turn left from the carpark and cross the nearby bridge. Just beyond it, turn left onto a road, which soon deteriorates to a track. Simply continue straight ahead for 5km (about 1 hour), there being only one point, after 1.5km or so, where you could make a mistake by forking left. The track takes you through a wide variety of scenery: fields, forests, lake and mountain in varied and wondrous combination (2). Beyond the end of the lake take the first turn left to reach Glendowan, where you should turn right for the kiosk or left for the road walk.

The road, which carries a modicum of traffic, is a somewhat inferior version of the outward route. Continue straight ahead where the main road swings right, turn left after 2km from here to pass by the Outdoor Pursuits Centre and the Colmcille Heritage Centre (3), and turn left onto the main road for the Gallery.

Notes

(1) Glebe Gallery contains works by among others, Picasso, Kokoschka and Jack Yeats. Beside it is the house of painter Derek Hill, which contains his wide-ranging collection of antiques and art works.

(2) About 2km along the track, on its landward side, are the pitiful remains of some of the houses associated with the Glenveagh evictions of 1861. After the murder of a steward, all 254 of the tenants on the estate were evicted and had to emigrate to Australia.

(3) This Centre gives an interesting history of the life and times of this well-known local saint.

ROUTE 7: MUCKISH

Muckish (666m), from most angles looking like an upturned boat, is unmistakeable. Its top is a plateau at least a kilometre long and from it its sides fall everywhere in steep ground, and here and there in scree and cliff. The northern approach, the main route given here, should be approached with care in bad weather. Leave time to wander around the summit plateau.

Getting There From Creeslough take the N56 towards Dunfanaghy for over $1^1/_2$ miles to turn left at a graveyard on the right (also a good reference point from Dunfanaghy). Drive straight ahead for about 3 miles to a point where a grassy track crosses the road and park around here (GR 009309). This is an old railway line, as you will see by looking right, where there is a cutting. **Buses** Swilly Bus, McGinley's or O'Donnell's to the graveyard (so to speak).

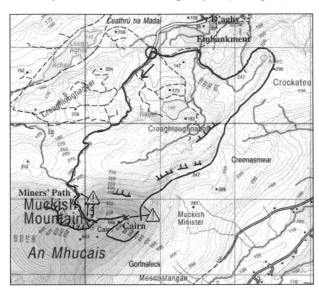

Walking Time 4 hours (distance 9km, climb 680m), including about a half-hour over Naismith for the steep descent from the summit.

Difficulties The Miners' Path up the cliffs near the start demands full attention – and a clear day. The descent from Muckish may cause navigational anxiety in bad visibility.

Good underfoot conditions to Muckish summit, after which some soggy ground.

Map Sheet 2.

Route From the parking place walk onward and upward on the road (soon a track) until you reach two sets of foundations at the foot of steep ground and cliffs. These are the old sand loading bays (1). Walk to the upper one and to its right across a narrow stream you will see a path, the Miners' Path in fact. The idea now is to follow this path, higher up partly marked by posts, directly upwards to a quarry. It is most important to keep to this path; there are one or two places where cul-de-sacs can lead you astray and it is easy to do this in bad weather. So off you go and when, at length, the path crosses a sand-filled gully you can breathe easily again as you are nearly there.

'There' is the quarry from which the quartzite sand used to be extracted. It is a place of some wonder: rusting machinery and crumbling buildings, light-brown rocky pinnacles fronting quarry walls and more than likely a fluttering raven croaking aloft. Let's move on.

It's only a short climb from here to the summit plateau. If you stand facing out at the quarry edge, the path to the summit, which is roughly indicated by metal posts, is on your right and winds up over no more than moderately steep ground. The path peters out near the plateau, but at this point all is simple, with the summit trig pillar (not marked on the map) close at hand at about GR 005287 (1.75 hours).

As already said, it is worth while taking time to wander round the summit plateau. The views in all directions are excellent, Muckish's northern cliffs magnificent and the terrain, gently sloping with one huge cairn in the centre and numerous boulders scattered and heaped everywhere gives easy walking.

Now for the descent. The steepest feasible point (feasible for some, anyway) at which to descend eastward is from the cairn built on unusually well-constructed foundations about 150m east of the trig pillar. You can make a less steep descent over heather by walking a few hundred metres south-west from this cairn. Descend steeply from here for very roughly 200m (height) and then contour left to pass below scree until you are directly beneath the eastern tip of the summit plateau. From here you can walk to the crest of Muckish's north-east running spur. This is not the most elegant of descents but, unless you are into the scrambling required of the direct descent, it has the virtue of keeping body and soul firmly together.

The next objective is Crockatee (295m), over 2km away to the north-east and reached by keeping high ground and the occasional stretch of cliff close by on the left. Along here you may come across a group of tree stumps sticking out of the bog, a relic of the times when all this area was forested. Further away on the left you can admire the huge areas of boglands around Lough Naboll, now being extracted for fuel.

From the northern summit of Crockatee the plan is to circumnavigate Lough Akeo, keeping to the higher ground so that you are shortly walking south-west with the lake behind you. Then descend to the outlet stream from Lough Akeo, which you should meet by coming off the right of the higher ground. Follow this stream to the old railway embankment (it looks at first like an improbably massive dam for the tiny stream). Climb it and turn left. This gives you an elevated route across the bogland right back to the nearby start. Here and there along the embankment you will come across the grassy remains of the old sleepers and can perhaps visualise the tiny engine chugging its way to far-off Burtonport.

Easy Variation It's an easy climb from Muckish Gap to the summit plateau. The Gap (GR 999268) is the highest point on a minor road about 6 miles south-east of Falcarragh and about the same distance south-west of Creeslough, and is marked by a shrine. From there simply follow the rough path north-east for about 500m (distance, not climb) then north-west and north to reach the summit plateau. Take care that you come down at about the same point, as there is difficult scree to the west in particular. Walking time is 1 hour to the near edge of the summit plateau.

Notes

(1) Fine-quality quartzite sand used in the manufacture of spectacle lens was quarried here until 1955.

(2) Looking back from the Miners' Path you can see the grassy embankments of the Letterkenny and Burtonport Extension Railway. Opened in 1903, it was intended to help the fishing industry in Burtonport. Never a commercial success, it was closed in 1940. ■

ROUTE 8: HORN HEAD

Marvellous sea-cliff scenery on a peninsula facing Tory Island, with good views landward towards Muckish and Errigal. This is an easy walk, but you can easily lengthen it by walking right round the peninsula on the long variation outlined below.

Getting There From Dunfanaghy take the road signposted for Horn Head. Keep straight ahead for over a mile, then turn left uphill signposted 'Horn Head Scenic Drive'. Turn right at the tee, still following this sign, but keep straight where the Drive indicates a right turn and park at the end of the road (GR 014409). **Buses** Swilly Bus, McGinley's, or O'Donnell's to Dunfanaghy.

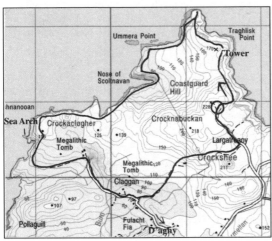

Walking Time 3.75 hours (distance 12km, climb very approximately 350m). (It is difficult to judge total climb in an area where climb can be so easily traded for distance.)

Difficulties Some high vegetation but not normally wet. No navigational problems.

Map Sheet 2. Note that contour lines have been omitted in depicting sea cliffs.

Route From the parking place it might be worth while climbing to the nearby ruins of the look-out post simply for the view and to get an idea of the route. Then head east, firmly ignoring easy paths heading in not quite the right direction. When you get close to cliffs and steep ground, keep them on the right and walk! This course will take you past the ruins of the Signal Tower and on to Horn Head itself where you can cross a fence to get a better view. From here the chief feature seaward is Tory Island to the west, lines of headlands and inlets to the east, while to the south rise a whole set of mountains of which Muckish is by far the most prominent, with Errigal much farther away to its right. A wide range of birds, not all of them sea birds, nest and breed on or near the 190m high cliffs here.

They include kittiwakes, guillemots, puffins, peregrines, choughs and ravens.

Continue along the cliffs past an extensive slice of moorland and onto the headland beyond it. You can walk as far as you like but I suggest you start to head for home after you have seen the impressive Templebreaga Sea Arch which lies nearly 4km (1 hour or so) from Horn Head. You will first see it when you are a little past it; from it walk another few hundred metres along the coast and here follow a neatly built stone wall roughly east to the nearest farmhouse.

Close to it you will meet a track onto which you turn right to make your way through agricultural hill country. After about 1km cross a stream in a hamlet and turn immediately sharply left onto a narrow track. Along here look out on the right for a grass-topped hill near at hand (it's Crockshee (211m)) because you will be walking with it on your right. For the moment keep to the track until it swings sharply right to service the one farmhouse on it and then leave it to walk north-east along the shoulder of the hill behind this farmhouse.

This course will take you into rough hill country sheltering the sad ruins of a few houses and remains of abandoned fields. Crockshee is now near at hand and if as suggested you keep it on the right you will meet a track that will shortly take you to the road. Turn left on it for the nearby start.

Long Variation Park on waste ground just beyond Hornhead Bridge. Walk the road onward and where it swings left uphill take to the beach. Keep to the beach for at least 1km until you are past a stream issuing onto the beach, as there is impassable vegetation inland before this. After that all is navigationally easy: just keep the cliffs and steep ground on the right.

Walk to the near end of Tramore Strand, which you cannot fail to notice since it is at least 2km long. From here a spot of compass work may be needed, aiming across the sand dunes to reach the northern side of Hornhead Bridge. Later, keeping forest on the left you should to pick up a track ending at a gate by the bridge. On the road turn left for the car or right for Dunfanaghy.

The walking time is 6 hours (distance 17km, climb about 470m), including some time for difficult terrain.

Note

Horn Head peninsula was once an island. Sand was blown from the west to form a bridge to what is now the peninsula, as you can see from the sandy terrain between Dunfanaghy and here. Older maps show the lake, now significantly called 'New Lake', as an inlet of the sea open to the west. ∎

ROUTE 9: AGHLAS

The three graceful cones of the Aghlas, rising from broad Lough Feeane, lie between Errigal and Muckish. All three offer excellent views of both peaks, as well as further afield. From the north they form a memorable and what is more a natural circuit, the latter a rarity in this area.

Getting There From Falcarragh take the road south from the village centre, that is turn left from Dunfanaghy, ignore a minor turn on the right after 0.4 miles and turn right after another 0.7 miles. Fork left uphill after another 2.6 miles and after another 1.4 miles park just past the fish farm gates on waste ground (GR 936258). This point can also be reached from Gortahork. **Bus** Swilly Bus, Mc Ginley's or O'Donnell's to Gortahork (6km).

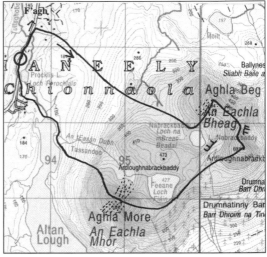

Walking Time 4 hours (distance 9km, climb 700m).

Difficulties Boggy terrain in the lower ground but otherwise excellent. Easy navigation.

Map: Both sheets 1 and 2 with an awkward changeover.

Route Walk back along the road from the parking place to cross the nearby bridge. Take the first turn right to a farmhouse, if necessary ask permission to go on, and beyond it climb gently south-east using what tracks you can find to reach the shores of Nabrackbaddy Lough. This initial stretch to the lough is definitely the most boring of the entire route, so you will doubtless be pleased to reach the lake and contemplate the trio of fine peaks rising from the lake shore.

The first climb is a direct one through occasional patches of scree to the huge cairn on Aghla Beg (564m, 1.75 hours) from where the view is magnificent, encompassing a wide range of lovely mountains in nearly all directions.

The second of the Aghlas lies over high, easily traversed ground to the south-east. This Aghla (603m) is unnamed on the maps. In spite of this cartographic indignity the views from this, the highest of the Aghlas, are just as good as from Aghla Beg. The descent is through peat-hag country towards the large Lough Feeane. From close to the shores of the lake the ascent to Aghla More (584m, 2.75 hours) is obvious, a stiff one at this late juncture.

From the small cairn on Aghla More a little care is needed on the descent to avoid scree on the south-western and northern sides. Walk initially at about 310° compass from the small summit cairn, and after a few hundred metres you can veer right to reach easier ground and eventually the shores of Altan Lough, where slow progress ensues through difficult haggy ground.

Walk to the northern end of Altan Lough where you may cross by fording the river close to the lake or at the stepping stones a little further on (wet feet may result, though at this late stage it should not be too discomforting). Take the track running north along the opposite shore. This ends at a gate where you turn right onto the road to reach the nearby parking place.

Variation from the South Not a good natural circuit and with some dull ground to be traversed (twice!) but convenient if you are staying south of the Aghlas. Start at the Altan Farm pillar on the R251 (GR 952205). Take the track from here to the shores of Altan Lough, climb Aghla More (2 hours), descend east to reach the western shore of Lough Feeane, walk south of Nabrackbaddy Lough and then follow the main route to Aghla (603m), descend to Altan Lough. Walking time is 5.25 hours (distance 13km, climb 980m).

Youth hostel Variation If you are staying in Errigal youth hostel you might get a Swilly, O'Donnells, or McGinley bus from around Gweedore to Gortahork, climb Aghla More (3.25 hours), descend to the eastern corner of Altan Lough and take the track from there to the R251. **Map** Sheet 1. Walking time from Gortahork is 5.75 hours (distance 18km, climb 750m).

Muckish Gap to R251 Variation The central and longest section of the annual Glover Highlander Marathon Walk is an exhilarating walk with much the same characteristics of the main route above. **Maps** Sheets 1, 2.

Start at the shrine at Muckish Gap (GR 999269). Keep forest on the left to ascend to the plateau of Crocknalaragagh (pts 461m, 454m) where the small lakes are better landmarks in exceptionally soggy terrain than the nondescript 'peaks'. Descend to the shore of Lough Aluirg and keeping it on the left, cross its outlet stream and climb the spur to the south-west to near the summit of Aghla Beg. Climb Aghla Beg (2.5 hours), Aghla (pt 603m), Aghla More, descend to the eastern corner of Altan Lough. Take the track running from here to reach the R251 at Altan Farm pillar (GR 952205). Walking time is 5 hours (distance 12km, climb 930m). ■

ROUTE 10: SLIEVE SNAGHT AND THE POISONED GLEN

The quartzite dome of Slieve Snaght dominates the Derryveagh Mountains, whose rocky crest is riven by low, transverse, parallel cliffs. This austere country gives some of the most rewarding walking in Donegal. The route options are many but this one taking in the Poisoned Glen is probably the best of an excellent selection.

Getting There In Dunlewy drive past the youth hostel on the left and take the next turn right signed 'Poisoned Glen'. Park at the hairpin bend just after the derelict church, where there is plenty of room (GR 929189). If you are staying at the youth hostel there is an attractive walk to this point (route 2). From the east take the R251 to Dunlewy, turning sharp left at the sign 'Poisoned Glen'. **Bus** Swilly, O'Donnells, or McGinley bus to around Gweedore.

Walking Time 4.75 hours (distance 12km, climb 710m).

Difficulties Easy underfoot until near the end when much boggy ground has to be endured. In good visibility no navigational difficulties especially with the huge cone of Errigal across the valley to act as a constant landmark. In bad weather navigation is much more difficult particularly in the Rocky Cap area.

Map Sheet 1.

Route From the start you can see most of the route, prominent among which is the silvery dome of Slieve Snaght rising amidst expanses of bare grey rock. An awe-inspiring sight!

Walk down the road from the church to take the track at the nearby hairpin bend. This leads across a bridge and from there you can follow the stream on the right into the Poisoned Glen. As you advance over level, boggy ground the grey rocky walls of the Glen close in on all sides, apparently leaving the inward route as the only escape. Not so. The ascent route, evident for much of the walk into the Glen is to the distinct lowest point in the cliffs ahead.

So, when you reach the end of the valley cross the stream and, from a solitary tree, climb directly upward initially through heather, keeping cliffs closer on the right than the left as you ascend. Near the top the climb is steepest but not vertiginous, so you should arrive in good spirits on level ground overlooking Lough Atirrive Big (1.5 hours).

The stretch from here to Lough Slievesnaght to the south-west is a difficult one navigationally in bad weather. It consists of an undulating climb over a flattish peak known locally as Rocky Cap (over 580m), followed by a steep descent to the lake, this progress punctuated by a series of low crossways dykes (1), some of which shelter tiny lakes. After the two indeterminate summits of Rocky Cap, your advance to the south-west is abruptly terminated by the north-south cliffs which mark its western end. Some of the slabs of vertical rock around here form rough rectangles (one is cantilevered over the void); these are as good an indication as any of the imminence of the cliffs.

It is best to approach the northern end of Lough Slievesnaght from the north-east where a grassy ramp aids the descent to this large lake, a good setting for a rest. From here it is a straight climb to Slieve Snaght (3 hours), which is crowned by a well-built cairn set in a wide plateau of short grass. From it you should easily see Errigal (north), the Aghlas to its right and Muckish farther right with the large Aran Island off to the west, and that's only a selection.

Descend south-west from Slieve Snaght to a wet area at a col, though it is hardly wet enough to merit the lake shown on the OS map. This direction avoids cliffs to the west, but the snag is that there are many boulders to be negotiated, so it may be better to veer right into steeper but easier ground. From the col or near it descend north to reach the right bank of the Devlin River.

From here on all is simple navigationally but soft ground underfoot makes for rough going, especially initially. On this long descent do not follow the Devlin River slavishly, as at one point its route resembles that of a demented ant: here you can make a short cut across moorland. Nearer Dunlewy the river has cut an impressive gully in which trees shelter: the scenery here is much more memorable than upstream.

As you near the road you will readily see that you will have to cross two streams on the right in order to reach the initial and only bridge of the day. After that it is a short walk to the start.

A Less Boggy Variation If you want to avoid the worst of the bogland of the main route start this variation at the col north of Lough Slievesnaght. Descend initially north but gradually veer north-west to keep as long as possible to the high ground to the west of Lough Maam. On this course you will eventually reach the boggy banks of the Devlin River.

An A to B Variation Leave one car at the junction at GR 019248, that is 7 miles north-east along the R251 from the start. **Maps** Sheets 1 and 6 and, if you are ultra-cautious, you might also take sheet 2 for a tiny section at the end. Follow the main route above to climb the cliffs of the Poisoned Glen (1.5 hours), walk east to cross the deer fence in a tiny cliff-bound valley, continue east for 500m, then swing north to descend to Lough Beg (GR 9518), climb Maumlack (GR 958189, 3.5 hours). (Most of the rest of the route is described under route 13.) Walk over Edenadooish to Dooish (5 hours). Continue north-east to Saggartnadooish and pt 391m, climb Kingarrow, cross the deer fence to reach the road junction. Walking time is 6.5 hours (distance 15km, climb 1080m).

Note

(1) These mark the lines of igneous dykes. Hot magma was thrust up vertically from the bowels of the earth and pushed aside the existing rock. The cooled magma is less resistant to erosion and has been worn away quicker than the pre-existing rock, hence the dykes.

ROUTE 11: SLIEVE SNAGHT FROM THE SOUTH

If you are staying south of the Highland area it may be more convenient to tackle Slieve Snaght from the R254, which runs on the south-east of the Derryveagh Range. This approach is not so rewarding as from the north but is still an excellent circuit.

Getting There The start is about 13 miles east of Dunglow. Take the N56 towards Glenties, turn left onto the R252, in Doocharry take the R254 for 5 miles to the carpark at Lough Barra at GR 929124.

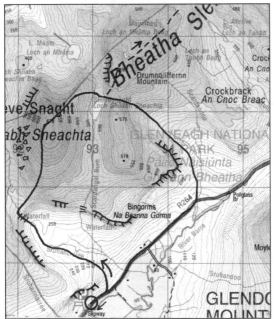

Walking Time 4 hours (distance 9km, climb 640m), including some time for boggy terrain.

Difficulties Navigation generally easy. Terrain good in higher ground but very wet lower.

Map Sheet 1.

Route Walk north-east along the road, that is onward from the Dunglow direction, to round a line of cliffs. After a few hundred metres you will be able to take to the soggy ground to the left. The idea here is to push north-westwards towards the waterfall at the end of the valley, so do not confuse it with the one that comes into view first and which is on its northern side. This is a very wet stretch and it might be as well to keep above the valley floor as it is marginally drier.

Climb with the waterfall on the right, keeping clear of the long slabs on this side if you feel nervous - they are more intimidating on the other side. At the top of the waterfall you can veer rightwards away from the stream and climb through boulders to the solid cairn on the top of Slieve Snaght (678m, 2.25 hours).

From Slieve Snaght descend on its north-east spur, and near its end veer right off it to walk to the northern end of Lough Slievesnaght. From here - and this is the only point in the route where the terrain is of no help in route finding - head directly east for less than 1km (say 10-15 minutes) to cross a low ridge. Once in, or at the side of a soggy valley, head south-east to reach the road, and turn right on it to reach the parking place over 2km away.

Errigal and the Aghlas (Routes 9, 12)

A to B Variation Without a second car, for every kilometre on the mountains you will have to walk one on the R254 which is scenic but also quite unvarying. With two cars however you can leave one about $2^1/_2$ miles further north-east from the start given above, where there is room for careful parking along the road. Take the main route to Lough Slievesnaght, climb the grassy ramp directly to its north-east to reach the indistinct rocky plateau of Rocky Cap, descend to the top of the Poisoned Glen north of Lough Atirrive Big. From here turn south-east, keeping to the high ground east of that lake so as to avoid extremely wet ground in the valley bottom. Walking time is 4.25 hours (distance 9km, climb 850m). ■

ROUTE 12: ERRIGAL FROM THE NORTH

The usual approach to Errigal (751m), the most distinctive mountain in Ireland, is from the south, but this more unusual approach is through varied (but not everywhere interesting) terrain. After climbing the mighty scree-sloped cone the route traverses two less distinguished peaks before returning along the shores of Altan Lough. A fairly tough but enjoyable route.

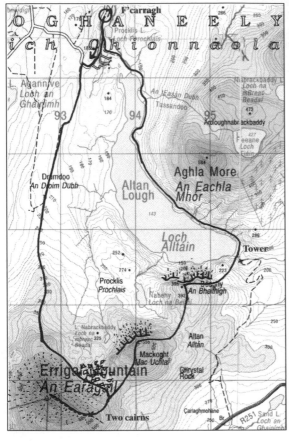

Getting There The starting point is the same as route 9.

Walking Time 6 hours (distance 15km, climb 850m) allowing a half-hour over Naismith for rocky terrain. However this time is even more approximate than usual because the time taken on the steep descent from Errigal varies greatly from person to person.

Difficulties Some soggy bogland and boulder-hopping. Navigationally not too demanding.

Map Sheet 1.

Route Walk onward for nearly 1km to cross a stile on the left and walk the track beyond south through moorland. This is the dullest part of the route, though the views east to the Aghlas and Altan Lough are magnificent. After a long 3km, and here Errigal dominates the skyline ahead, the track comes to an end, leaving the weary traveller to carry on without it.

Still southward-bound, the slope finally steepens and the ground underfoot becomes somewhat drier. At length you will reach the scree slope itself, where you will have to judge for yourself whether to attempt the direct approach to the summit (see below). If you decide against it, keep to the left of the high ground to enter the edge of a fascinating area of rocky hummocks lying between the base of

Errigal and nearby Mackoght. This is not an area where you can make quick progress, unless you do not mind risking a crocked ankle.

Climb the ridge of slabby rocks at the southern end of the hummocky area, and on its crest swing right to reach two cairns marking the stony path to the summit, the only easy way of reaching it. This path takes you into a terrain of extensive scree slopes dropping straight from the heights. It's a navigationally simple vertigo-free progress; within 5–10 minutes of its end at the summit you attain the crest of a ridge where the path is marked by a set of cairns, into one of which is set the Joey Glover memorial.

The summit, probably the smallest in Ireland, consists of two tiny peaks about 30m apart, joined by a narrow ridge. It is a superb viewpoint, with the mountain's surrounds seemingly at your feet and much of Donegal and beyond within view. Slieve Snaght, the huge dome to the south, and the great line of hills stretching on both sides are the most prominent, but on good days you can easily recognise Benbulben in Sligo, its right flank falling precipitously to the plains.

Retrace your steps from the summit to the two cairns noted earlier and then follow the rocky ridge all the way to Mackoght (555m). In poor visibility this is a difficult summit to find, as it has a few similar rocky high points, each with a cairn. However, what is unmistakeable are the steep scree slopes along its northern side. Carefully avoiding these, descend initially east for a few hundred metres and then climb north to the bogland forming the undistinguished hump of Beaghy (395m), watching out for scree slopes on *its* northern side. Beaghy's one attraction is the excellent view it offers over Altan Lough, with the Aghlas towering behind.

From the summit descend east, so rounding Beaghy's hazardous northern side and then swing north-east to cross a narrow stream close to a curiously remote tower set in abandoned fields at the eastern end of Altan Lough. Navigational problems, such as they were, are now behind because all you have to do now is walk the north-east shore of the broad lake. There is a path most of the way along the shore, traversing the narrow ground below Aghla More. Apart from scree slopes reaching to the lakeshore at one point, it gives moderately easy walking for 3km. When you reach the northern end of the lake you should be able to easily wade across as the river is wide though shallow. On the far side you will pick up a track which ends on tarmac. Turn right for the nearby start.

Adventurous Variation If scree slopes hold no terror for you it looks feasible, though I haven't tried it, to climb directly to the Errigal's summit from the north.

Tourist Variation You can climb Errigal from the south-east starting on the R251 0.5 miles west of the gate pillar for Altan Farm (easily missed!) and 1.6 miles east of the side turn right (as you drive east) signposted 'Poisoned Glen'. There are several other places along the road west of the Altan Farm pillar where you can park and which are almost equally good starting points.

Climb to the summit initially following posts to find the path up the south-east side. Walk the main route to the tower on Altan Lough; here take the track back to the R251 and turn right for the start. The walking time is 4.5 hours (distance 8km, climb 680m). ■

ROUTE 13: DOOISH

At 652m, Dooish is the highest but not a particularly dominant peak in a lengthy line of bare and rocky mountains, stretching north-east from Slieve Snaght. The route starts at Lough Beagh, focus of Glenveagh National Park (1), and takes in the spine of this north-eastern end, including of course Dooish itself.

Getting There Before you go there, read note (1) below. The entrance to the Park (GR 0323) is well signposted from all directions. It is about 7 miles south of Creeslough and about 14 miles north-west of Letterkenny.

Walking Time 5.25 hours (distance 15km, climb 570m).

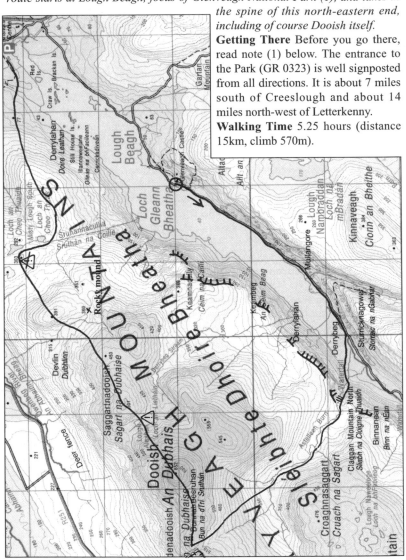

Difficulties Lots of wet ground. Navigation is not too difficult except that there are long stretches without distinct features and this may be more than disconcerting in bad conditions. Mistakes are not dangerous but take care not to wander into the steep ground north-west of Lough Beagh. If all else fails head for the R251 to the north-west.

Map Sheet 6. The *old* National Park one-inch sheet, which you might get at the Park entrance, is acceptable.

Route From the Castle walk between the outbuildings to reach a clear track which runs for about 3km along the south-east shore of Lough Beagh, a track that offers excellent views of the lake. At the lake's end, continue for a short distance to a cottage on the left and here cross a footbridge on the right over the Owenveagh River. Then set your sights on the majestic Astelleen Waterfall close by across the narrow valley.

There is no easy way of reaching the waterfall: the intervening ground is always wet and the tussocks make for hard going. At length, though you may doubt it at the time, you will reach the foot of the waterfall and ford the stream below it. Next climb by the side of the waterfall (the ascent is easier with it on the right); you will probably have to veer away from it near the top to avoid crags, though the ascent is not perilous.

At the top of the waterfall you find yourself in a high, bare, gently sloping valley. Follow the stream north-west for about 1.5km, where the main stream veers sharply to the right as it descends. Here climb steeply, at last out of soggy country and into more rocky terrain, north-west to Edenadooish (521m) (2). You might note that in bad weather the high deer fence, whose direction changes by over 90 degrees between the two summits of Edenadooish, is a good landmark.

Turn north-east from Edenadooish to face the stiff climb to Dooish itself, the goal of the route. Crowned by a well-built cairn and with cliffs on its northern face, Dooish (652m, 3.25 hours) commands good views especially towards the Errigal-Muckish range, views that are enhanced if you walk to the cliffs.

Drop steeply from here to Lough Aleahan. You will see from the OS map (but it is not so evident on the National Park map) that there is a long narrow cleft starting just south-east of the lough and running parallel to the general south-west to north-east trend of the range. (Incidentally in the floor of the cleft is a small rocky mound (pt 360m at GR 003222) which may be a useful landmark in bad weather.) Keeping to the north-west of this cleft, cross the bare rocky erratic-strewn plateau of Saggartnadooish, and continue over similar ground to climb pt 391m. From here descend to Misty Lough North and South in turn, both of which snuggle in wet country south of Kingarrow.

From here to the Visitor Centre the object is to keep as far away from Lough Beagh as possible, as the nearer to the lake you walk the wetter the ground and the higher the tussocks. At length you will reach a gate at the western edge of a mature wood. From here, it is a short stroll by track back to the Centre.

Notes

(1) From September to February inclusive, if you intend to leave tracks and paths you must get permission from the Park authorities as there is likely to be deer culling during this period.

There is a small charge into the Park. Cars must be left at the Visitor Centre (GR 039232).

From there the bus, when running, will take you to the Castle (GR 020209) where the route starts. The bus runs only in summer. At other times you face an additional walk of 3.5km.

The Visitor Centre has a great deal to interest the outdoor person. The Castle and its gardens, a formal space in the midst of wild splendour, is also worth a visit.

(2) Around here you can see the first of the straight line dykes which run across the grain of the mountain range nearly as far as Slieve Snaght. There is more about this under route 10.■

ROUTE 14: THE KNOCKALLA RIDGE

The 5-km long, narrow Knockalla ridge almost spans the Fanad peninsula and gives easy walking with expansive views in none too wild surroundings, there being agricultural land on both sides. It is impossible to make a good circuit out of this configuration so the choice is a 4-km walk on narrow roads at the end of the walk (main route) or the bus to make an A to B route (variation).

Getting There From Carrowkeel/Kerrykeel (GR 2132) take the R247 for 1.6 miles to park at the junction of the R247 and the road to Glenvar, where there is

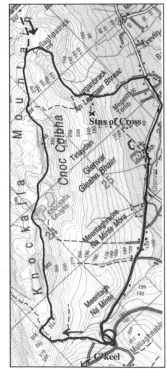

room, a few metres down the Glenvar road, for several cars (GR 236330). **Bus** Swilly Bus to Carrowkeel, but see also the variation below.

Walking Time 3.5 hours (distance 11km, climb 420m), including the 4km road walk at the end, which takes about an hour.

Difficulties None.

Map Sheet 2.

Route Walk back to the junction of the R247 and the Glenvar roads and here take the track on the right rising into heathery country north-west towards the Knockalla ridge. Keep on this track until it runs out close to the summit of pt 318m and then, using whatever sheep tracks you can find, climb through high heather to the top.

From here there is a steep drop to the col facing pt 311m. Among the boulders around here you can easily find specimens of geographical lichen, recognisable because it looks remarkably similar to a map depicting political boundaries. Incidentally from the col onward you will be into a terrain of rock slabs, boulders and short vegetation, a great improvement on the wearying heather of the lower ground.

There's little to be said about the navigation from here on: simply keep to the crest of the ridge over pt 363m (GR 2334) and then walk down to the two large Knockalla Loughs. It's debatable whether you should keep these on the right or the left, but to avoid the bog roads hereabouts, whose tentacles are spread much higher than shown on the map, it might be best to keep them on the right and cross two minor hummocks on the way to pt 363m (GR 2435).

You can walk a few hundred metres north from this pt 363m, still on rock and short grass, before making a decision. Here you can shorten the route by swinging right (east) off the main ridge to meet a track or you can continue along this ridge to face the Urris Hills across Lough Swilly. Since the route is not long or demanding it is just about worthwhile extending it though there is wet ground ahead. If you so decide, walk about 1.5km north-east along the main ridge until you see two lakes in somewhat lower ground to the right (they are not shown on the OS map), walk to them and climb tiny Callaghpatrick (226m) beyond them. Then keeping a shallow and wet valley down on the right walk south until you hit the track mentioned earlier, which provides an easy route to tarmac (it's part of 'The Way of the Cross', a traditional Catholic custom). From there turn right and walk a wearying 4km back to the start.

The Cliffs at Glenlough (Routes 37, 38)

Bus Variation. To avoid the road walk take the 1110 hours (but check times) Swilly Bus from Carrowkeel and alight at the crossroads at GR 2338 near Portsalon. Walk roads from there generally south-east to reach the coast road running south-east of Stocker Strand. After the second hairpin bend take to the hills and walk generally south-west keeping roughly to the crest. At the end continue along the crest past pt 381m to pick up a track close to Carrowkeel and from its lower end walk into the village. Walking time is 4 hours (distance 12km, climb 580m). ■

ROUTE 15: CIRCUIT OF GLENTORNAN LOUGH

The sizeable Glentornan Lough lies south of Dunlewy and the mountains around it form the western extension of the Derryveagh Mountains. Though underfoot conditions are squelchy in part the easy walking along the higher ground culminating in Crocknafarragh (517m) and the view into the lough and across to Errigal and Slieve Snaght make this an enjoyable walk.

Getting There Follow the sign for the Dunlewy Centre from the village of Dunlewy (GR 9020), continue past it to cross the causeway between Dunlewy Lough and Lough Nacung Upper, and park carefully along the road at the first convenient point beyond the causeway (probably about GR 902188). If you do happen to drive over a bridge before you park, note it as it is important for the start of the route. **Bus** Swilly Bus, McGinley's or O'Donnell's to near Gweedore.

Walking Time 4 hours (distance 10km, climb 560m), including less than a half-hour over Naismith for rough terrain after Glentornan Lough.

Difficulties With several indeterminate summits on the route, particularly near the start, not the easiest area to navigate over, though the large Glentornan Lough is an excellent landmark. Since there are only a few short stretches of cliff in the area, mistakes should not be dangerous. Much soggy ground lower down.

Map Sheet 1.

Route Cross the first bridge after the causeway and ascend by the stream here that cascades impressively into Lough Nacung. You will shortly have to make a decision, one that frankly I am unable to. Especially in bad visibility it may be easier to follow the stream for about a half-hour to a level area and then head west with a touch of south to reach Lough Croragh, the first landmark. However you may be happier to veer right from the stream near the start and instead follow the crest of an indeterminate spur south-west to this lake. The smooth slabs on its east side provide a good spot for a rest.

From Lough Croragh head south over further indeterminate ground, from where you should get your first view of the great dome of Slieve Snaght to the south-east, a far from indeterminate peak. However less than 1km south of Lough Croragh you will encounter the first peaklets of Crockglass (in turn pts 456m, 471m, 489m and 464m). They lie in a graceful arc, and all of them except the last have beds of small, sharp stones on and around their summits. If you get confused in this area of many similar peaks you might note that there is a mighty split boulder just east of pt 489m.

Point 464m, the last of these peaks, is not strictly necessary for the route, but since it gives good views over Glentornan Lough and the country behind and ahead of you, it is worth taking in. Beyond it cross a shallow valley to the south-west to climb the first of the two peaks of Crocknafarragh (517m, 503m), which while not exactly nondescript, is none too 'descript' either.

However, do not worry too much about getting lost, because between the two low peaks of Crocknafarragh is a lake at least 100m long. This is Lough

Mullincrick and a useful starting point for the next leg of the route. Follow the outlet stream from this lake towards Lough Glentornan, thus avoiding on your left an awesome expanse of gently shelving bogland spilling northwards in sombre brown raiment. As you approach the latter lake keep to the high ground curving left parallel to its shore, so avoiding a steep drop if you attempt a direct descent.

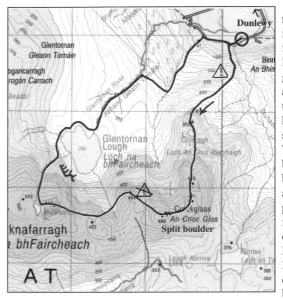

Eventually you will reach the shore and with it on the right, pass a few beaches, one of lovely fine sand, thus giving a good excuse for a rest. After it walk to the outlet stream, and keeping it on the left, start off downstream. The problem here is bogland, so there may be much climbing up and jumping down from peat hags and sinking into the water-logged courses between. After less than 1km from the lake the river has cut a deep channel into the bogland: quite an impressive sight. About here you will be close to an impenetrable forestry plantation, so there is nothing for it but to turn right away from the stream and make your way parallel to the forest. After a few hundred lengthy metres you will be close to a corner of forest and will be able to cross another stream ahead, this one also set in a channel, though a shallow one. Walk directly downhill to the road, and turn right here for the nearby start.■

A large peninsula flanked by two long inlets to east and west, Inishowen has neat and attractive villages, pleasant wooded areas and a superb coastline.

The hills of Inishowen bear the south-west to north-east imprint of the Highlands, though less firmly. The highest point is bulky but mundane Slieve Snaght (615m) (route 20), though the narrow line of hills to its north-west, centred on a steep, winding road through the Gap of Mamore (routes 17-19) offers much better walking. There is also much good walking to be had along the rugged, remote, indented coast (routes 16, 21), especially that to the north facing out towards Scotland.

Map Sheet 3.

ROUTE 16: DUNAFF HEAD

An easy walk around Dunaff Head, which gives excellent rocky coastal scenery with - and this is unusual for sea cliff walks - a convincing looped route. There are lovely flowers in summer, especially at the start of the walk.

Getting There The start is in Dunaff, which is neither well signposted nor, as a scattered settlement, is it easy to recognise even when you reach it. From Clonmany (GR 3746), 4 miles away, cross the bridge out of the village, and here set your milometer. Turn right, fork left at 1.2 miles, fork right at 2.2 miles. Shortly after turn right at an off-set crossroads, turn right at 3.7 miles, after which you should pass a post office on the left. Turn right at the nearby tee and park near the end of the road (GR 324486).

Walking Time 2 hours (distance 6km, climb about 250m).

Difficulties Mostly rough but generally dry ground underfoot. No navigational difficulties.

Map None necessary but take sheet 3 if you have it. It does not show the cliffs adequately.

Route Continue onward to the shore and turn left onto it to walk along the beach until you are past a nearby tiny harbour. Then start to climb along the tops of the developing cliffs, passing an impressive inlet as you ascend. At about the first major island, Bothanvarrra, the ground tends to level and the cliffs assume a more rounded, grassy profile. At this island therefore, you can elect to climb to the first of the cairns on the rough ground forming the summit of Dunaff and reach the cliffs again farther along.

At the inlet beyond the grass- and lichen-covered second island, you may decide to walk down towards the sea, now bordered by low cliffs and rocky inlets. If so you might note that you will have to climb about 50m towards the end to surmount a final section of cliff. Past this section, cross a low waterfall issuing directly into the sea and keep fences on the left to reach a small, stony beach. Take the track at this beach to reach tarmac, turn right onto it and left at the nearby tee. Walk less than 2km on road to the start. ■

ROUTE 17: BULBIN

The bare grassy hill of Bulbin with its rugged rocky ribs to north and south is easily climbed and provides an excellent viewing point in all directions.

Getting There Cross the bridge out of Clonmany (GR 3746), and at it set your milometer. Turn left immediately, turn right uphill at 0.9 miles, and park at about the junction on the left at 2.1 miles (GR 358435).

Bus Swilly or North-West Bus to Clonmany.

Walking Time 2 hours (distance 5km, climb 350m).

Difficulties Some wet ground, otherwise good. Navigation is easy, but beware of the short stretch of cliff on the north side of the summit that is not adequately indicated on the maps.

Map Sheet 3, though hardly needed.

Route Walk onward along the road, which eventually deteriorates to a stony track and curves in a gentle arc round the western side of the mountain. After about 2km from the start the track levels out on the south side of the mountain amid boggy, higher ground on both sides; it is time to take to trackless country.

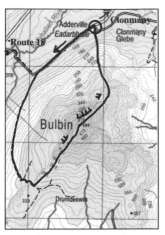

So, turn left off the track and climb directly to the summit, a steep rocky slope on the left and the summit memorial increasingly obvious ahead. The summit itself is a good standpoint from which to study the mountains on both sides of the Gap of Mamore westward and the Slieve Snaght area in the south-east, as well as a wealth of coast and other mountains. The memorial, built to commemorate the Eucharistic Congress of 1931 has a receptacle claiming to contain holy water. If so, it must attain holiness on its downward passage as secular rain!

Keeping a wary eye on the cliffs to the left keep onward and downward from the summit, veering left to keep to the high ground when safely past these cliffs. You can reach the 'main' road on which you started walking by using one of the several gates fronting this road. Don't attempt to reach it to the left of the one and only house along here, as there are young trees there. ∎

ROUTE 18: RAGHTIN MORE

This is the northern end of the narrow range of hills which reach the sea, as the Urris Hills, at Dunree Head. A walk along a wooded defile is followed by dreadfully wet bogland before you reach the rounded but drier uplands, which offer superb views over mountain and coast. The entire range may be easily walked with the use of a second car.

Getting There Cross the bridge out of Clonmany (GR 3746), turn right immediately, and drive for 0.8 miles to park in the 'Waterfall Carpark' on the right (GR 359469). **Bus** Clonmany is served by Swilly and North-West Buses, from where the route may easily be walked.

Walking Time 4.5 hours (distance 11km, climb 820m).

Difficulties Much wet ground in the lower, flatter areas. Navigation is generally easy.

Map Sheet 3.

Route Walk a few metres farther along the road and here follow the signs for the waterfall. This will take you up a track and then down into the heart of a narrow, wooded defile, Butler's Glen (it's some 'glen'!), on a well-built path that crosses the defile's stream over and back a few times before coming to an end at the low but impressive waterfall.

Climb steeply out of the defile, keeping the waterfall on the left and head directly west through wet country to Raghtin Beg (416m), and then with

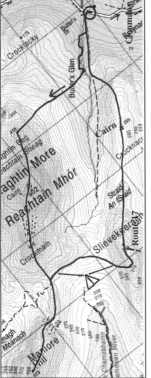

scarcely a drop to the summit of Raghtin More (502m, 1.75 hrs). It is crowned by a huge cairn and a trig pillar (their positions are reversed on the map).

Most of the hard work is now done, so you can advance quickly past a long sinuous lake to climb or by-pass the occasional scree slope on the way to Crockmain (460m). The next target is Mamore Hill. To get there, drop fairly steeply from Crockmain into boggy country scarred by corrugations of turf workings, picking a line to the left of the direct one to cross two rocky hillocks. This will take you to the foot of a path that traverses the steep ground ahead and avoids the extensive scree that guards this approach to Mamore Hill.

Mamore Hill (423m, 2.75 hours) is highly attractive; it gives even better coastal and hill scenery than that enjoyed all the way from Raghtin Beg while its top, consisting of a narrow, rocky ridge plunging southwards towards the Gap of Mamore, is the best in the entire area. It's well worthwhile to walk to the last of several cairns on the summit.

Retrace steps down the scree slopes to face a dull section facing Slievekeeragh. Here you have the choice of descending into a boggy valley to reach the top of the ridge south of the summit or attempting to contour around this valley to reach the same point, the latter route being marginally the easier. On the top of the spur, walk north to Slievekeeragh, and continue north to pass a fine square cairn on its northern top (299m). From here you can descend towards Butler's Glen again, picking up a clear track, the lower portion of which you walked at the start.

Longer Variation Descend from the summit of Slievekeeragh to the road junction at GR 346432, here taking the track running east, the leftmost one (it initially looks like a driveway to a house) and then picking up route 17. You can follow this route all the way to Clonmany (and the bus) or the Waterfall Carpark. Walking time to the carpark is 6.5 hours (distance 18km, climb 1180m).

A to B Variation To combine this route and route 19, walk south from Mamore Hill to the Gap of Mamore, taking care on the steep narrow spur. Veer left off the spur as you approach the road to meet a rough track, the start of route 19. The second car should be parked at about GR 298399. This point may be reached by driving from Fort Dunree (GR 2838), and forking left twice. The second fork, onto a narrow road, crosses a bridge and then climbs steeply. There are several places to park uphill beyond the bridge. Walking time is 4.5 hours (distance 10km, climb 1020m). ■

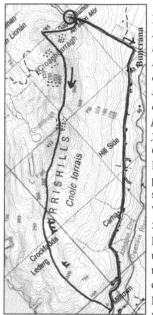

ROUTE 19: THE URRIS HILLS

If one walk must be chosen in all Inishowen, this is it. A steep but short ascent from the Gap of Mamore leads to a high, narrow, rocky ridge, enlivened by a switchback terrain of closely spaced ups and downs. Unfortunately the walk is all too short and the return, along minor roads is pleasant but not spectacular. With a second car, you can combine this route with route 18.

Getting There Start around the top of the Gap of Mamore (GR 319430), which is fairly well signposted from both directions and where there are several places at which to park a few cars.

Walking Time 2.75 hours (distance 9km, climb 520m).

Difficulties Getting to the crest of the ridge is easy unless visibility is poor; once there the route is navigationally simple. Generally good underfoot conditions.

Map Sheet 3.

Route Walk to the south side of the Gap and a few metres on take an encouragingly level track on the right. Sadly, you must leave it almost immediately to climb steeply west with a touch of north to the easily seen cairn on summit 365m. Now more or less on the main ridge drop slightly south to get definitively onto it. Once attained the route ahead is clear and the views all along here magnificent. A short section of high ground is followed by a couple of dips with short but steep scree-sloped climbs between. The second climb ends at the highest point in the Urris Hills, pt 417m. If there are any lingering doubts about this point, the two lakes backed by a bony ridge, Crunlough and Fad, on the right of the ridge should dispel them.

From this point follow the high ground in a gentle leftward arc, steep slopes close on the left. Though it isn't critical, you might meet a fence paralleled by boundary stones, running roughly south-east as you descend; this you can follow to the road (1.5 hours). Turn left here, walk steadily gently uphill through remote country for over 3km, turn left at the tee and walk steeply uphill to the start.

Warning! In an attempt to provide something new for you, dear reader, my wife and myself attempted to reach the coast north-west of the Urris Hills ridge and walk back along the sea cliffs. Don't try it! It's a nightmare of hidden rocks, high heather, bracken and scree. Only the 2km or so immediately south-west of Lenan Bay is walkable. ■

ROUTE 20: SLIEVE SNAGHT (INISHOWEN)

Slieve Snaght at 615m is the highest point in Inishowen but is surrounded by stupendous areas of gently shelving bogland. A long haul during which the panorama reluctantly, but finally triumphantly reveals itself, ends on an outlier of Slieve Snaght and from here to the descent from another outlier, there are good views and fairly rugged terrain.

Getting There Park in the village of Drumfree (Drumfries on the signposts) (GR 3839), about 5 miles north of Buncrana on the R238. **Bus** Swilly Bus and North West Busways run services to the village.

Walking Time 4.25 hours (distance 12km, climb 700m).

Difficulties Lots of high vegetation and wet ground. Navigation is easy in spite of the gently sloped terrain in the lower ground.

Map Sheet 3.

Route Take the R244 (Carndonagh road) to turn first right onto a track and walk it for about 500m. Here the track swings sharply right at farmhouse. Walk a few more metres and then turn left onto another track to cross a wide but shallow stream. Continue along this track for a short distance. With new forestry looming threateningly ahead turn right off it and head to Slieve Main, towards which a rough compass bearing of about 120° may be no bad idea in this area of near horizons and subdued peaks.

You may have to make a few detours as you advance to avoid fences and new forestry. Otherwise there is nothing to impede progress and nothing much of interest in the terrain apart from two unexpectedly steep climbs near the summit. However the gradually unfolding land- and seascape should help keep your mind off the mundane ground underfoot.

The summit of Slieve Main (514m, 1.75 hours) is quite flat, with patches of boulder field here and there and a few small cairns, any of which could mark the highest point. The wide panorama, unbroken except in the direction of Slieve Snaght, is some reward for efforts so far.

We must now turn our attention to this mountain. Head directly to a col to the north-east of Slieve Main (you can avoid the worst of this col by walking south-east from the summit and then heading on the crest of high ground to the col).

From it climb directly and quite steeply to the summit, heralded by an area of rock slabs, most lying horizontally, but with the odd vertical one, thus giving the impression in cloudy conditions anyway of a particularly gloomy graveyard.

Slieve Snaght (615m, 2.75 hours) has a circular stone shelter surrounding its trig pillar. As befits the highest point in all Inishowen, the views are wide. As

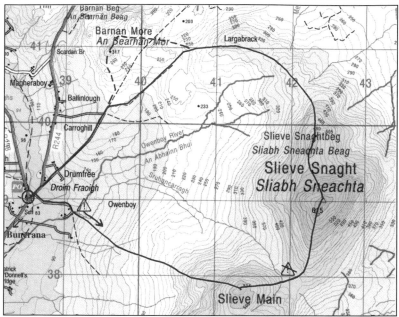

well as most of the mountains of Donegal, Rathlin Island and some of the Hebrides and the Paps of Jura can be seen in good weather.

The descent is directly north over Slieve Snaght Beg. Make sure here not to mistake a subsidiary cairn on a slight rise for the summit cairn, 200m or so farther on. From Beg head north-west over broken, boggy terrain, keeping to the higher ground. To simplify navigation head roughly for the craggy crown of Barnan More on this erratic and slow descent.

When you reach a bog track (and linear rubbish dump) all you have to do is turn left and keep walking straight ahead to Drumfree. Before you head for the start however, you might like to consider a short extension to Barnan More. Its steep-sided flanks of shattered rock are a sharp contrast to the bogland here-abouts and it overlooks a lovely area to its north. From its summit you will have to get back to the bog track only a few hundred metres south to avoid upland fields but the detour is still worthwhile. ■

ROUTE 21: THE NORTHERN CLIFFS

Of the several stretches of coastal cliff in Inishowen this is probably the best, with offshore islands, sea stacks and low but impressive cliffs. This is a there-and-back walk, but you can make it into an A to B (see below). However, with dull gently moulded bogland inland a looped walk is not recommended.

Getting There Park at the 'Wee House of Malin' (GR 433582) off the R242. To get there take the R242 from Malin village for about 6 miles, continuing straight ahead at Mullin's shop where the R242 swings left. Drive directly to the nearby

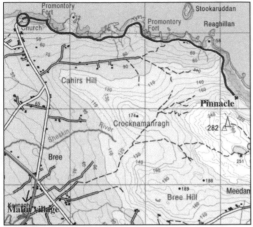

seashore, where there is limited parking.

Walking Time 2.25 hours (distance 7km, climb 250m).

Difficulties Some rough ground but otherwise easy. No navigational difficulties.

Map Sheet 3 but hardly necessary.

Route Walk eastward along the impressively wild storm beach and near its end after a few hundred metres, climb one of several narrow grassy gullies. At its top you will see that any other route would lead across fences or through a ploughed field.

Fences still lie ahead and you should keep to the seaward side of them as best you can. However there are only a few and beyond them you can concentrate on the powerful coastal scenery: the Garvan Isles riding close in, Inishtrahull (the northern-most point of Irish land) beyond and an increasingly dramatic line of sea-cliffs, with two sea arches off-shore.

Also ahead looms the imposingly cliff-bound, partly lichen-covered island of Stookaruddan. The cliffs rise for about 1km beyond Stookaruddan, reaching their highest point in this section at a phallic-like and easily recognisable pinnacle (1.25 hours). The grassy land beside this pinnacle is the recommended turning point if you intend to do a there-and-back walk. It is a marvellous eyrie, with a wealth of sea, mountain and coastline scenery to behold, including glimpses on the far horizon of the Scottish island of Islay and the Paps of Jura over 100km away.

The only consolation about returning by the same route is that you do get a new perspective on the scenery, unless of course you have been looking backwards most of the time on the way out!

A to B Variation The total walking time for this variation is about 3.5 hours (distance 10km, climb 360m). Return transport should be left at Glengad about 7 miles away at about GR 515545. At the end try to keep to the cliffs for as long as possible to avoid bog roads that have been used as rubbish dumps. ∎

Rocky Cap Mountain (Route 10)

Directly north of Donegal town are the Blue Stacks, whose indistinct peaks are at about 600m and whose highest point is only 674m. The whole range is protected by formidable foothills to the south, through which the occasional impressive waterfall tumbles, and by even more formidable stretches of bogland on this side and to the north. Curiously, although this is a most remote area, it is not inaccessible, at least from the south, which is within a few miles of Donegal town.

The core of this mountain range is the area round Lough Belshade (routes 25, 26). This large mountain lake is edged, particularly to the west and north by some of the most wild and untamed country in Ireland, so that Belshade itself is a most useful and unmistakable feature.

This central Blue Stacks are not an area in which to wander in bad weather, for, while there are only a few stretches of cliff, they and the numerous crags in the area are most intimidating if their full extent cannot be judged. To get some idea of their grandeur without the attendant risks try Banagher Hill (route 22), in the foothills to the south.

The area east of the central Blue Stack area, abutting the traffic-laden N15, is also rocky and wild, but a lot wetter. These are the Barnesmore Mountains (routes 24, 28), which extend to the area south of the N15, where recently erected wind power turbines have not improved the scenery.

To the west of the central Blue Stacks there is an abrupt change from bare rock to a vegetated and much wetter terrain. In this area the two highest peaks are the Lavaghs (671m, 650m) (routes 25, 27), lofty but rounded summits. The Lavaghs overlook the Sruell Valley (route 27), a lovely area poised between the rocky and boggy sections of the Blue Stacks. Further west of the Lavaghs the Blue Stacks peter out in boggy, grassy hills separated by inhabited valleys (route 30 below).

To the north of the Blue Stacks are areas of low hills that are not so good for walking. In this region the most impressive hill is Aghla Mountain (593m) (route 23), just to the south of hill-bound Lough Finn, which shares some (only some) of the characteristics of the best of the Blue Stacks.

Map Sheet 11. ∎

ROUTE 22: BANAGHER HILL

A forest track before and a road walk after the rough ground on the plateau of Banagher Hill (392m), where the numerous lakes form a pleasant foreground to the views of the nearby Blue Stacks and Lough Eske.

Getting There The start is about 4 miles north of Donegal town. Take the N56 towards Killybegs from the centre of the town, turning right after a few hundred metres at the sign for Harvey's Point Hotel. Drive onward for over a mile, where there are churches to right and left, and turn gently (not acutely) left here. Turn right after another 1.9 miles and park at the forest entrance on the left after 0.6 miles (GR 937826). **Bus** All local bus services serve Donegal town (see the Introduction). Bikes may also be hired in the town.

Walking Time 4 hours (distance 14km, climb 350m).

Difficulties Few navigational problems. Nonetheless I admit to getting lost on the plateau, admittedly in horrendous circumstances, which goes to show that there is no perfectly safe mountain area. Lots of rough ground on the plateau.

Map Sheet 11.

Route Take the forest track through forest that allows good views back over Donegal and its bay. After you glimpse Banagher Lough through trees on the right you reach shelving unforested moorland, still on the track. After another half-kilometre or so through this moorland the track begins an unsteady descent. Here you are confronted by a fence across the track, a small clump of trees on each side and dense forest looming beyond. Time to leave the track's sanctuary and head into the wilderness

The next task is to find Lough Cam to the north-east, the largest lake on the

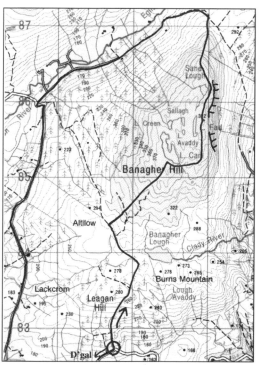

plateau. To do so, initially follow the fence uphill to the right of the track but where it shortly swings left continue on a compass bearing to the lake, which presents a generous target. On this leg you may come across a cairn just to the west of the lake, or in the same area the occasional spherical boulder bulging with stony warts, pustules and pimples - not a pretty sight.

From Lough Cam you can wander at will on the lake-studded plateau, so the following is only one of several possible routes.

Walk east to the edge of steep ground overlooking Lough Eske and then turn north to pass Lough Fad and Sand Lough. Descend north, keeping a fence on the left to reach the road. On this descent the contrast between the rocky (right) and grassy Blue Stacks (left) is most striking.

On the just-about road turn left and walk through quite a variety of wood and field punctuated by the occasional lonely homestead that seems to have almost succumbed to the forestry around it. At the 'main' road turn left. Unless you have arranged for a car you now have at least 5km on road to the start. But this long road walk is no great hardship; it runs high above the partly wooded, hummocky valleys of the Eglish and Sruell Rivers and gives excellent views of them and the sea further away. Don't forget to fork left at the two junctions on this road or you may find that it is even farther than you had bargained for! ■

ROUTE 23: AGHLA MOUNTAIN

In an area of dreary, gently sloping soggy mounds, Aghla Mountain (593m), with its rocky escarpments, deep gullies and tiny knolls of shattered boulders, offers good variety.

Getting There The start (at GR 890006) is just off the R250 about $2^1/_2$ miles south-west of Fintown and 7 miles north-east of Glenties. From Fintown drive the length of Lough Finn and take the first left shortly after it. Park on nearby waste ground. From Glenties take the R250, keep on it where it swings sharply right with a minor road straight ahead, and turn next right. **Bus** McGeehan's to the start.

Walking Time 3.5 hours (distance 9km, climb 520m).

Difficulties A modicum of wet ground but generally OK. The navigation is not the easiest after the summit of Aghla where there are stretches of cliff and crag, but none that can't be easily evaded.

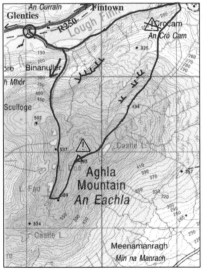

Map Sheet 11.

Route: Take the track along the shore of Lough Finn and you will immediately see forestry rising up the hillside and two deep gullies before it.

The one sustained climb of the route is now at hand, one which offers many opportunities to admire Lough Finn – and to get your breath. Climb directly along the near side of the nearer gully, until you are high above the top of the forestry at a tiny fork in this gully. Here walk south over more level but soggier ground, the object being to find the first of a line of lakes running parallel to the summit ridge of Aghla itself. After finding the first the rest should be easy to find. Along here the views west are excellent: you should be able to pick out Aran Island to the north-west and the mighty bulk of Slievetooey to its left.

At the first lake you have still five to find, all but one (it is slightly offset) in a north-south line. The last, and smallest, the one you must find, is preceded by a distinct climb and has scree above its left shore. By the way, if you are wondering: there is no reason at all why you shouldn't walk along the summit ridge just to the east. The only reason for this route is that it avoids a there-and-back.

From this last lake climb to the cairn at the southern end of the summit ridge (pt 589m) and then walk north along its rocks and outcrops. From here the rumpled Blue Stacks are close by to the south-east with lower and blander hills to the east. To the north are the more striking hills of the Highlands, with the dome of Slieve Snaght particularly evident. Walk to the northern summit (593m), whose trig pillar the Ordnance Survey people seem to have mislaid, since it is not marked on the map. (Still on the defects of the map, note that the forestry marked close to Castle Lough, soon to be encountered, does not exist.)

Glengesh (Route 35)

From the trig pillar walk initially north-east to nearby Castle Lough, from where you are perfectly placed to walk down Aghla's north-east spur, a rocky one similar to the summit ridge. The map shows that you really want to end up on the spur to the left, but the spur you are now on is higher, more distinct and gives better views. However once committed to this spur do not change your mind as there are short but nasty crags to negotiate if you try to reach the other.

As you reach the end of the spur you will find that you will probably have to negotiate a few minor crags anyway. After this, cross a stream and head for the last echoes of the spur you did not walk, at this point a few bumpy, grassy hills. At their end you will reach a track and should turn left onto it.

The rest is easy. Follow the track along the scenic shores of Lough Finn, partly through forest, many of whose trees have been downed in a storm. At its end you will hardly be surprised to find yourself with the initial gullies close on the left, Lough Finn still on the right, and with only a short walk to the start. ■

ROUTE 24: THE BARNESMORE MOUNTAINS

The glacial valley of Barnesmore is bounded on the north-west by the Barnesmore Mountains, which give lovely views of the heart of the Blue Stacks. They are surrounded by intimidatingly wet lower ground, and though the higher land is partly rocky, there are also wet areas here. One advantage of the Barnesmores is that it lends itself to several variations that can be made on the trot.

Getting There The start is at one of two adjacent rough lay-bys on the right of the N15 (from Donegal town, 9 miles away) just north of the Barnesmore Gap (GR 042872). Watch out for the prominent Barnes Bridge (not signed) and prepare to cross the road (a fast one) shortly after. If you don't fancy this manoeuvre, you can park at the forestry entrance on the left about 0.3 miles beyond the bridge, where there is room for only a few cars. Coming from the opposite direction start slowing down at the large electricity line crossing the road. **Bus** Table 290 Bus Eireann service or O'Donnell's. A bus is essential for the A to B variation, assuming only one car.

Walking Time 4.25 hours (distance 10km, climb 540m). This allows about 45 minutes over Naismith for slow progress through soggy ground.

Difficulties Lots of wet ground lower down, However, there are no more than a few short stretches of cliff in the area, so mistakes should not be serious.

Map Sheet 11.

Route Walk the track from the forestry entrance on a gradual climb through low trees. After about 1km it swings sharply right away from Barnes Lough, which is visible down on the left. Continue on the track for a few more minutes until you have passed the forest boundary fence. Leave it here to climb north-west to Brown's Hill (498m), passing on the way its cairned south-eastern top.

Brown's Hill, in spite of its modest height, commands good views to the north and west with Gaugin Hill, its left flank forested, near at hand and Slieve Snaght, Errigal and flat-topped Muckish much farther away in north Donegal. From the summit cross a flat, reedy, muddy col to the west and after that you can wander at will, maybe taking in all three indistinct peaks of Croaghnageer, which give excellent views of the nearby rocky and rumpled central Blue Stacks to the west. However perhaps the most elegant circuit is to take in summits 521m and 571m of the trio, crossing a north-south ditch on the way between the two. This ditch is a shallow, natural indentation carrying short grass, running in a long and undeviating line; it might be a modest navigational reassurance.

Summit 571m (2.5 hours) is immediately preceded by a north-south oriented lake about 100m long, another modest reassurance. From the summit head roughly south aiming to descend on the crest of one of a few rocky crag-sided spurs separated by deep-set streams, an area glorying in the name of the Tawnawully Mountains. As you approach the headwaters of the Barnes River, you will see a waterfall across the valley, a suitable route to Croaghconnellagh should you choose to climb it (see below).

If you don't, you face a tiring slog through high and usually wet ground. Turn left at the valley bottom and plod to Barnes Lough, which is just over a kilometre away, though it seems much longer.

Walk the length of the lough (it also seems inordinately long), cross one narrow stream and continue roughly east and uphill to reach the track on which you started. Kissing the ground will be excused! Turn right here and walk the kilometre back to the forest entrance. Turn right for the lay-byes.

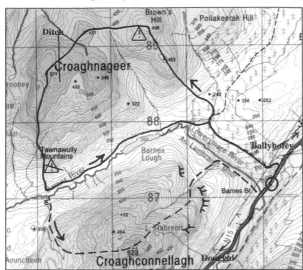

Croaghconnellagh Variation From the valley of the Barnes River you can climb Croaghconnellagh to the south-east, initially following the stream which disgorges into the valley as a waterfall. The ground becomes rockier and there-fore easier to walk as you ascend.

Descend north-east from the summit, from where there are two spurs. If you are on the eastern spur you will have to swing left off it as it ends in cliffs. There is a very rough path above the Lowerymore River and this may be some small help on the walk to the N15. Walking time from the Barnes River is 2 hours.

A to B Variation Walk to Croaghnageer as described above, climb Croaghanirwore to the west and then descend west to the Ulster Way near the headwaters of the Corabber River. Take the Way south to the road along the western side of Lough Eske and walk 10km on country roads into Donegal town (if you haven't arranged for a lift, of course). The total walking time is 7 hours (distance 21km, climb 640m). ∎

ROUTE 25: NORTHERN BLUE STACKS

The central Blue Stacks, though from a most remote starting point. This route starts and ends with a walk-in and walk-out over mostly wet boggy terrain, but the central section is an exhilarating walk over bare rock. A route that can be easily varied at both ends of its high central section.

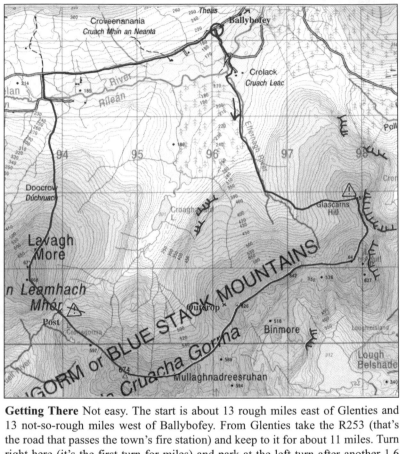

Getting There Not easy. The start is about 13 rough miles east of Glenties and 13 not-so-rough miles west of Ballybofey. From Glenties take the R253 (that's the road that passes the town's fire station) and keep to it for about 11 miles. Turn right here (it's the first turn for miles) and park at the left turn after another 1.6 miles at GR 960942 (there is ample parking).

From Ballybofey take the R252, keep straight on at the church after 4 miles where the R252 swings right, and now on the R253 (Glenties road) continue straight ahead for about 8 miles, turning left here (the second in less than a mile). Park at the left turn after another 1.6 miles.

Walking Time 5.75 hours (distance 16km, climb 950m).

Difficulties Good underfoot conditions except at the boggy start and end.

Navigation is difficult over much of the high ground. If you are in trouble simply head north towards the road, as there are only a few stretches of steep ground in this direction.

Map Sheet 11.

Route Take the side road south and cross a bridge serving a nearby farm. Then cross a bridge directly to the farm's right. Keep a fence on the right to ascend steadily southwards along a stream. After nearly 2km take the east fork where two tributaries meet and follow it for a while (the important fact to remember here is that you are going to climb Glascarns Hill on the east of the valley, so if you miss the junction it doesn't matter too much).

Eventually you must leave the safety line of the stream and strike out boldly through an increasingly rocky terrain for the summit of Glascarns (578m), crowned by an assemblage of massive boulders. Glascarns marks the start of the core Blue Stacks terrain to be enjoyed until the final descent: tough, predominantly rocky country with no definite peaks.

Turn south after Glascarns, cliffs on the left, to climb pt 641m (2 hours) whose only characteristic feature is Lough Aduff just to its east. Not much of a landmark, though considerably better than anything for the next few kilometres.

The next task is to find your way across the heart of the Blue Stacks, as I have said before a region with no definite peaks but with erratic rocks, huge slabs of granite and shattered boulders to contend with. Basically the task is to reach summit 674m, nearly 4km away to the south-west. On the way you will climb summits 642m and 626m at each end of a stretch of high ground, and then descend into lower ground before climbing summit 674m. There are two navigational aids on this long tricky leg. One is the ubiquitous Lough Belshade, the other the huge white unmistakable (yes, really unmistakable) outcrop 200m west of summit 626m. With these two good landmarks .... you can still go wrong!

In spite of the symbol on the map, there is no trig pillar on summit 674m (3.5 hours), the highest point in the entire Blue Stacks. This summit marks the transition from rocky to grassy terrain and the end of navigational difficulties. From summit 674m walk north-west to the top of the Sruell Gap, where there is a sturdy wooden post. From there it is a stiff climb to Lavagh More (671m), which has two minor peaks barely rising above the summit plateau. From the northern summit head initially north with a touch of east along a broad spur before descending north into wetter country, the aim now being to reach the bridge over the Reelan River (at GR 937933). Take care to avoid damaging fences on this descent.

Cross the bridge, turn right at the tee beyond it and walk a pleasant 2.5km to the start. On this stretch you can see the far-off white outcrop clearly if weather allows. Let's hope you could see it when you really needed to! ■

ROUTE 26: CIRCUIT OF LOUGH BELSHADE

The grey boulders and bare slabs of the central Blue Stacks are at their most austere in the area of Lough Belshade. Though without clear peaks, and with only one significant landmark in addition to Belshade itself, this is the best walk in the Blue Stacks and ranks with walks anywhere in Ireland.

Getting There From the centre of Donegal town, about 5 miles away, take the Killybegs road for a few hundred metres, turning right before a major roundabout on the N56 at the sign on the right indicating Harvey's Point Hotel. Follow signs for the hotel until it is signed 1km away, then continue straight ahead for 1.5 miles to a minor turn on the left. Take this for a few hundred metres to park on waste ground on the left (GR 956849). To avoid a road walk at the end you might like to leave a car at the end of the motorable road at GR 973870. **Bus** Bus Eireann route 480 and O'Donnell's serve the N15 (Donegal-Ballybofey road) and from there you can walk along either shore of Lough Eske. A bike might also be feasible.

Walking Time 6 hours (distance 17km, climb 740m), allowing extra time in the difficult terrain after Belshade Lough, counterbalanced by road walking.

Difficulties Don't venture into this area if visibility is likely to be bad, as there are so few good landmarks. If you are lost head for Belshade Lough, evading no more than short (but intimidating) stretches of cliff on the way. Quite good underfoot except for exceptionally soggy ground after Belshade.

Map Sheet 11.

Route The start is on a highly scenic minor (and deteriorating) road that traverses the high ground between Banagher Hill on the left and the Blue Stacks proper on the right. Take it through forest and then, about 2km from the start, into open, level country. Here turn right onto the second track on this side. At its nearby end you face the long but enjoyable climb into the heart of the Blue Stacks.

The idea here at the track's end is to reach summit 626m, nearly 4km away to the north. The scenery over most of this section is breathtaking: the grey slabs of the Blue Stacks in all directions and views behind over Donegal Bay and the Benbulben plateau beyond it. Do not let this distract from navigation. First there is a short bog-slog, followed by a steep climb through crags onto boulder-strewn gently sloping ground, possibly with a stream down on the right (it depends on your exact route). After which you face a search, not for the summit, a cairn on a far from obvious high point, but for an unmistakeable quartz outcrop only 200m or so west of it. Was ever, in a navigational desert, such a clear landmark placed so helpfully!

Having found the outcrop, walk to the summit (2.75 hours), which is in fact the south-west end of a high section of mountain and walk along it north-east for less than a kilometre to pt 642m, a cairned point but no more distinguishable than pt 626m. From here drop to a rocky col and climb pt 641m to the east. Once again an indistinct summit, were it not for the small lake just to its east, a modest enough landmark.

Time to start for home. Turn south, with the soggy valley of the Owendoo River far down to the left, to pass through pink sandstone slabs and reach a high col. It's a pity to have to record here that the route from here to a track 3km away is a tiring one through high heather or very soft ground. Anyway, turn right at the col to reach Belshade Lough (4 hours), situated in a lovely location almost surrounded by high ground which here and there steepens into cliffs over which cascades tumble. Turn left at its shore and walk to the outlet stream, crossing it on a rough dam serving a hydro-electric scheme.

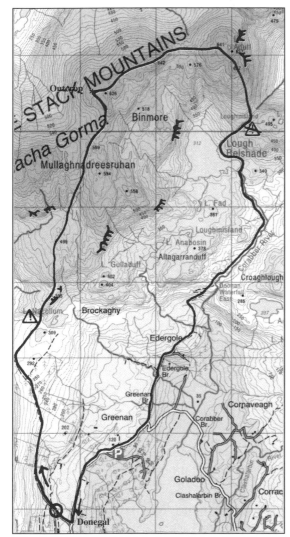

This is the really wearying stretch; even the scenery, rough hillside in all directions is only fair. Follow the stream to the main river, the Corabber, and continue downstream following it (and poles) until you reach the end of a track. Take it downhill, shortly cutting off a V in the track by taking a shortcut indicated by a post. On rejoining the track look back at the hills behind, rugged ramparts protecting the Blue Stacks proper, and at the breach through which the Corabber descends to Lough Eske by a waterfall partly hidden in trees.

After crossing a river on stepping stones you will reach a rough road and farther on the main road around Lough Eske. Continue straight ahead here (you might consider it a turn right). It's now a pleasant walk on road for 2km to the right turn where your car awaits. ∎

ROUTE 27: CIRCUIT OF SRUELL VALLEY

The magnificent Sruell valley, a steep-sided grassy glen dominated by cliffs on its northern side over which an impressive waterfall cascades, is the focus of this walk. It traverses part of the central Blue Stacks, crosses the head of the valley and ends between cliff and watery bogland on the valley's northern side.

Getting There The start is about 8 long miles north of Donegal town. From the roundabout on the N56 at the Killybegs side of the town take the Letterbarrow

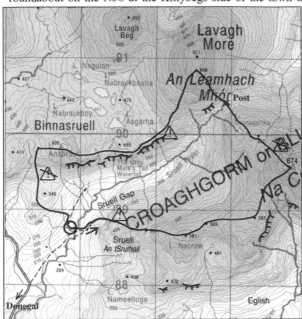

exit. Turn right after 2.0 miles, the second of two closely spaced turns on this side, and right again at a tee after another 2.3 miles. Drive onward to the end of the road, taking the right fork near the end where there may be doubt. (Incidentally, if you have more than two cars in the party it may be as well to park here at this fork, as the last half-mile of the road is narrow and parking is restricted.) Otherwise park considerately at the end of the road before the bridge to the right (GR 918886).

Walking Time 4 hours (distance 9km, climb 780m).

Difficulties From near the start you face navigational problems in an area without clear landmarks; after the head of the valley, it is soggy underfoot and although navigation is easier here you will still need care along the cliffs that overlook the north side of the Sruell valley.

Map Sheet 11.

Route Cross the bridge, walk past the front of the farmhouse, asking permission to go on if necessary, and walk onward past the outhouses until you see on the right a gate and track beyond it. Cross the gate and leave the track immediately to start a steep climb diagonally left upward.

From here on there are few landmarks but, in spite of this navigational headache you should be able to enjoy the scenery, with marvellous views over

Sruell and to the Grey Mare's Tail Waterfall across the valley and with a wider panorama opening up behind towards Donegal Bay and the Sligo hills.

Once you reach the crest of the spur attend to navigation. Keep to the crest to pass the insignificant pt 561m, a few lakelets at the col at pt 539m and then descend to a shallow col after the minor summit at pt 597m. This col marks a change in terrain: the predominantly boggy ground up to this yields to heaps of rock and minor slabs ahead, heralding the rocky core of the Blue Stacks. The grey lines of cliff on the right and reaching away eastward are also an indication of this sterner country.

Now you must find pt 674m, the highest point in the Blue Stacks and according to the Ordnance Survey, and they should know, crowned by a trig pillar. Except it isn't: instead there are two cairns on the rocky plateau (2 hours). If you can see the white quartzite outcrop 200m to the west of pt 626m this might be the best reassurance of your position. Except that you won't be able to see it when you really need it, that is in bad visibility. A hill walker's lot is not an easy one!

From pt 674m descend to the head of Sruell Gap to the north-west. Here you will find a clear indication of your position: a sturdy wood post. You can return along the wet floor of the Sruell Gap but if you decide to go on a stiff but straightforward climb of nearly 200m north-west to Lavagh More awaits.

Lavagh More (671m) offers fresh views on the Blue Stacks and westward to the long line of high ground that is Slievetooey, the golden strand of Maghera at its foot. More practically, you will see to the south-west a large area of soggy ground, evidenced by the lakes, large and small, scattered across it. The idea now is to keep this ground on your right and the cliffs overlooking Sruell on your left.

After descending south-west from Lavagh More you will pass a small lake wedged close to the cliffs. From here on it might be prudent to pay attention to navigation. Cross the hastening stream of the Grey Mare's Tail Waterfall, set in a steep, narrow valley. Then you face a modest climb, cliffs still close on the left, to a minor summit that shelters Lough Anabrack, whose reedy shores may be useful in identifying it. This lake is important to help in an easy descent back to the start. From it walk a few hundred metres directly west and then swing south, veering right if the ground is too steep for you. As you descend further head towards the farm where you started, picking up a track near it that will lead directly back to the start. ■

ROUTE 28: THROUGH THE BARNESMORE MOUNTAINS

A navigationally simple A to B walk that can be undertaken using the bus or two cars. It takes you through a remote and let's face it, wet valley in the heart of these mountains, with rugged peaks on both sides. The route in both directions is briefly described so you can walk it in whichever direction is most convenient.
Getting There If walking north to south, the starting point (at GR 043874) is the same as in route 24.

If walking south to north drive along the N15, turning off it to take the road along the eastern side of Lough Eske, pass a school on the right and begin the walk 1.9 miles farther on, at a cross roads (or maybe it should be called a crosstracks) at GR 984844. **Bus** You can get to either end of the route using the table 480 local Bus Eireann bus or O'Donnell's.

Walking Time Allowing about an extra 45 minutes for wet ground, about 3 hours if walking north to south (distance 8km, climb 160m) and a little more if walking in the opposite direction. In addition the road walk along Lough Eske is about 3.5km.

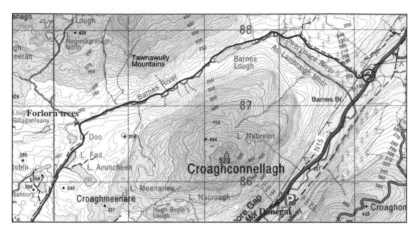

Difficulties The wet ground, already copiously alluded to, lasts for about 3km. Otherwise there are no navigational or other difficulties.

Map Sheet 11.

Route I will describe the route north to south and then give a few pointers to the opposite direction, the simpler navigationally.

Take the forest track uphill for about 1km (20 minutes). Here it swings right and you will have to find your way to Barnes Lough, which is visible from here, keeping young trees on the left. With the lake on the left walk to its end and far beyond, following the river in the valley, keeping close to it or above it, whichever you judge to be easier (a Hobson's choice).

Keep following what is finally a minor stream until – and this is navigationally providential – it unexpectedly swings left in its direction of flow at a few forlorn trees, leaving only a soggy trench in the direction you have been walking. Now head south for a few hundred metres and you will pick up a track. Turn right onto it and you will end up at the road circling Lough Eske (at GR 984844).

In the other direction, turn right off the Lough Eske road onto a narrow road (soon a track), as described under 'Getting There' above. Fork left at a lake at the one doubtful decision point, take it to its (the lake's) end, walk a short distance north across moorland to the infant Barnes River, take it downstream to Barnes Lough, and walk uphill roughly east to pick up a forest track. Walk to the N15. ∎

The West, as the term is used here, covers the coastal strip from Aran Island in the north-west as far south (and including) the great bulge of land reaching westward in south-west Donegal, which we will call, in the absence of any consensus as to its name, the Rossaun peninsula. The main feature of this whole region is the coast and the magnificent cliffs that protect the mostly hilly country inland.

As a comparatively distant off-shore island, Aran Island (so called on the maps - it is usually called simply Arranmore) is not the easiest place in the world to get to. However, if you happen to be there try to get to its western cliffs.

Further south the Rossaun peninsula offers a wealth of sea cliff walking. Starting at its north-east corner the sea cliffs west of Ardara are backed by the long ridge of Slievetooey (511m) (routes 32, 34) perhaps the one place in all this peninsula where the inland mountain is more attractive than the sea cliff itself.

Reaching west and south from Slievetooey as far as Glencolumbkille is a mighty stretch of cliff, off-shore island and sea-stack all of which is worth leisurely exploring in a navigationally simple area (follow the cliff edge!) (routes 37, 38). Apart from the difficulty of reaching it in a remote area with poor roads, the biggest problem here is to make a satisfactory loop in an area where much of the inland country is mundane and boggy.

South and east of Glencolumbkille the sea cliffs extend most of the way round to Slieve League (route 33), at once boasting the highest sea cliff and the highest peak in the whole region, both at 595m. Slieve League is a little 'upfront' in the sense that the whole sea cliff can be seen from one point, and that a carpark! Give me the more remote and unfrequented cliffs farther north. However it has to be said in Slieve League's favour that the inland-facing mountain gives good, easy walking - unusual for this area.

Now for the wholly inland areas. The valley of the Owengarve River (route 30) is really part of the 'boggy' Blue Stacks (see the previous section). Both Glengesh (route 35) and Crownarad (route 36) are similar in that they are centred on valleys, the former open, the latter forested. None of these three routes cover the most exciting hills in Donegal, but they offer fairly easy navigation on not too strenuous circuits.

Maps 1, 10. ■

ROUTE 29: ST JOHN'S POINT

The long narrow peninsula ending at St John's Point is worth a visit on a day of low cloud. This is a karstic area with outcrops of limestone which give it a slight overtones of the Burren though on a tiny scale. Take any road south from Dunkineely (GR 7676) on the N56 and drive to the beach about 5 miles away. From here it is well worth while walking to the end of the peninsula (it's only a kilometre or so) or you can wander along the road in the other direction. ■

ROUTE 30: CIRCUIT OF THE OWENGARVE VALLEY

West of the core Blue Stacks close to Glenties, is an area of generally subdued, grassy uplands that nevertheless encompasses small-scale rocky and cliff-bound country and manages to partly avoid wet moorland by using remote tracks. Though long, it can be easily made into two shorter routes.

Getting There From Glenties take the R253, which heads off the N56 at the small yellow and black sign reading N56 0292. After 5 miles park beside, or around, a school on the left (GR 891939). **Bus** McGeehan's or O'Donnell's serve Glenties, from where you might get a lift.

Walking Time 6.5 hours (distance 17km, climb 1040m).

Difficulties With a few distinct features navigation not too demanding. Apart from soft ground, the other problem is fences. At the time of exploring (October 1999) there are two to cross, but there may be more by the time you walk. *Find places where you can cross without damaging fences or yourself.*

Map Sheet 11.

Route Let's say you start at the school. Walk downhill, that is back towards Glenties, and take the third turn on the left, the one that runs at right angles uphill from the road you are on and has a house close to its right.

Walk this track on a gently rising curve that reveals the woods and fields of the Owengarve River valley and, at one point a section of impressive cliff, whose top we will reach later. After over 2km the track peters out beyond the last farmhouse, from where the climb roughly south to Silver Hill begins over soggy land. You can alleviate this sogginess by veering right from the direct route, thus not only gaining a rocky spur but also better views particularly towards the sea cliffs of Slievetooey and Aran Island to its right.

Silver Hill (600m) has a small lake on its otherwise undistinguished summit plateau. A line of lower boggy hills stretches out to the south-west while the two grassy Lavaghs rise directly to the east. The feature most evident from the summit however is probably the lakes sheltering on the semi-aqueous plateau to the south-east, whither, you might be glad to hear, we are not headed.

Our route instead lies to the north-east, a boggy col adorned with peat hags and reached over soft, grassy ground. From it climb north-east to the north-west spur of Lavagh Beg, passing on the way curious grassy hummocks spilling down into dreary bogland (there are more of these on the other side of the spur). The crest of this spur is marked by an east-west oriented lake about 15 double-steps long. Since it's not on the map, it not only serves to prove that I actually walked this route, but is a modest navigational reassurance in an area not noted for them. It is also the starting point for a there-and-back to Lavagh Beg.

From the crest of the spur you can take a partly rocky route north-east, thus avoiding moorland lapping its sides. The aim here is to reach the right of the last farmhouse on the cul-de-sac road in the valley, a farmhouse that gives the word 'remote' a new dimension. By the way, if you are puzzled: the map shows three major lakes in the area around the sources of the Owengarve and Reelan rivers. In fact there seems to be only one lake, the centre one on the map.

You should be able to reach the road to the right of the farmhouse without crossing fences. Walk away from it, turn left to cross the nearby bridge and walk

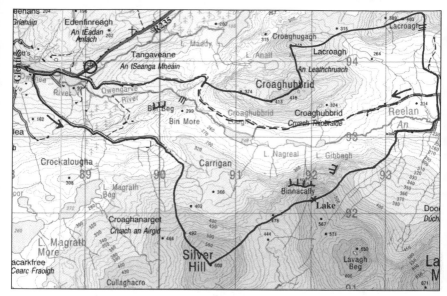

to a tee (3.75 hours). Here is a decision point: you can cut the route short by walking a track all the way back (see below). And before you decide, let it be said that the first part of longer route is dull, though it improves as you go on.

For the longer route, walk north on a track at this tee to an abandoned house. From here climb directly alongside a deep gash carrying a waterfall, above which is a sturdy white pole serving no evident purpose. Turn west at about the pole to climb pt 403m and continue west through uninvitingly rough country to the summit of Croaghugagh (410m), a low but rocky peak and the start of an area of small-scale but impressive features. Croaghugah itself gives excellent views to Aghla Mountain to the north, and to woods and lakes nearer at hand.

From here head south passing Lough Analf and make the short climb to Croaghubbrid, an east-west spur about a kilometre long with a terrain ranging from rocky outcrops to almost liquid bog. From the western end of the spur descend steeply but over grass to a track, here making a mighty vee through bogland.

All that remains now is to turn right onto the track, descending from high boggy ground to the east. Also descending, but more spectacularly, is the infant Owengarve, which tumbles in an impressive waterfall though rocky portals (you will see it if you look back). The track improves after 2km to a rough road that ends on the R253, where a right turn will take you shortly back to the school.

Short Variation Take the track through remote moorland, which is fairly dispiriting at first, but improves as you go on. The last part of this variation is described above. The walking time of this section is about 1.25 hours. ■

ROUTE 31: CROAGHEGLY

The rugged coastline of Crohy Head is backed by an upland area of low flat rocky ridges with steep scree-strewn sides. With the highest hill, Croaghegly only 245m high this is an area where you can wander without any fixed plan so that the following suggestion is only a framework for further exploration.

Getting There From the main street in Dunglow take the road west to Maghery, about 4 miles away, and park in the village (GR 7108). **Buses** Swilly Bus, McGeehan's or O'Donnell's to Dunglow.

Walking Time 2.75 hours (distance 9km, climb 320m).

Difficulties Some wet ground. With a road never more than about a kilometre away navigational problems should be minor.

Map Sheet 1.

Route Continue onward from the village on a narrow road giving views over a broad sweep of coast and ocean. Pass the youth hostel, and 1km beyond it ignore the fork on the right. About 5 minutes walking beyond, watch out for a minor road on the right heading steeply downhill at an acute angle, and take the track directly opposite it. Fork right after a few metres and continue upwards into mountain country to take the next track left, initially downhill. From here you can

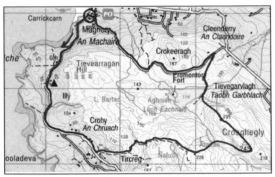

forget about directions for a while and concentrate on the scenery, rocky mountain ahead and a wild sweep of ocean behind.

The track rises onto the plateau and passes a small lake on the right, Lough Nafulla, beyond which it peters out close to an indeterminate top, pt 226m. What is not indeterminate however is the next target, the summit of Croaghegly (245m) to the east, as the trig pillar on the top is clearly visible from here.

To get there descend steeply north-east to the southern shore of Lough Atallan and from there tackle Croaghegly from the pass to its south-east, thus avoiding scree slopes guarding a direct approach. Walk along the hummocky ridge north-westward towards Aghnish Lough and turn right onto the track running along its near shore. After less than 1km, you will join a major track. Turn left onto it and it will lead you down into Maghery.

Variations The map will readily suggest other routes in this area. For instance you could walk farther along the road to pass two viewing points and then walk north-west along the entire ridge of which Croaghegly is the highest point. Or you could visit the lakes in the valley south-west of the Croaghegly ridge, or walk by road around the entire group of hills. ■

ROUTE 32: VALLEY OF THE OWENREE RIVER

This short walk takes in the long glacial valley of the Owenree River and varied remote country to its south. Though nearly all on track or road, the remaining short distance is still significant, as it is through difficult bog.

Getting There Park in the carpark just before the starting point of route 34 at the foot of Assarnacally waterfall (GR 669902). **Bus, bike** See under route 34.

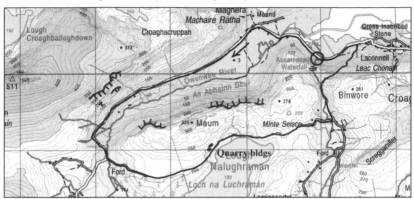

Walking Time 3 hours (distance 10km, climb 250m).

Difficulties None except for 1km through soggy and rutted bog (see the variation).

Map None necessary but take sheet 10 if you have it.

Route After admiring the waterfall, whose upper reaches you will observe later, walk onward along the road to the hamlet of Maghera. Continue for over 2km along the length of the Owenree River valley, at first gently and then steeply upward, on a barely motorable road offering widening views to an indented coast between the cliff-bound sides of the valley.

At the highest point of the road turn left off it onto a track traversing bogland, and at its indeterminate end continue east across the bog already alluded to, with forest close on the right. If it's any consolation the first part is the worst. At length you will be walking along the shores of the large but unimpressive Lough Nalughraman and you will see a slate quarry, apparently in the middle of nowhere above the shores of the lake. Walk to it to pick up a track. This leads across a bridge, on the other side of which are a few houses, a surprising sight in an area so seemingly remote. Turn left at these to take a track parallel and close to a stream swiftly flowing between steep and rocky banks, the upper reaches of the waterfall seen at the start. The track takes you to a lovely viewpoint high above Loughros Beg Bay, where you have an aerial view of a strange area of mudflats between sea and road. On tarmac again turn left for the nearby start.

Variation To avoid the sogginess of the main route climb Maum (325m) and then descend from it to about the slate quarry. This should take about 15 minutes extra. ■

ROUTE 33: SLIEVE LEAGUE

The sea cliffs of Slieve League (595m) are partly renowned (I am guessing) because it is possible to view the entire line of mighty cliff without walking more than a few feet from your car. The highest point of this line is at the summit of Slieve League and is an easy walk. You can of course return by the same route but the inland one described here gives good views over the corrie holding Lough Agh.

Getting There The start is about 14 miles west of Killybegs. From the town take the R263 to Carrick, turn left in the village, and right at the sign 'Bunglas/The Cliffs' near the post office in Teelin, and *not* at the sign for Slieve League just before it. Continue to the end of the road at GR 558757, passing through a gate on the way. Take it easy on the last section of road where there are steep gradients and acute bends. **Buses** Bus Eireann route 490 or McGeehan's to Carrick.

Walking Time 4.75 hours (distance 13km, climb 770m).

Difficulties None, except for the mildest of vertigo on the so-called 'One Man's Pass'. Navigation easy and underfoot conditions generally good though quite muddy on parts of the ascent.

Map Sheet 10.

Route If you have a cliff on one side and a path under your feet, as you have on Slieve League, there is little point in describing the route in pernickety detail. Simply take the path upward from the parking place and follow it. After pt 435m, a minor bump, you can, if you wish, keep to the rocky crest of the ridge, otherwise take the perfectly safe, but muddy, path winding round to its right.

At length you will reach the eastern summit of Slieve League (over 570m) marked by numerous cairns on a plateau of soft ground, with similar ground, (your return route, if you choose it) reaching away eastward. But for now the route is westward over the aforementioned 'One Man's Pass', which is simply a narrow level path with steep grassy slopes on both sides. Past this is the goal of the route, the trig pillar on Slieve League (595m, 2.25 hours). This is a marvellous viewing point with Benbulben to the south-east, the tiny but high Stacks of Broadhaven off the Mayo coast to the south-west and perhaps the cone of Errigal to be seen off to the north. It's worth walking a little further on to see the Chimneys, a group of high stacks on steep ground seaward.

Slieve League (Route 33)

And so to the return, which is certainly different in character and nothing like as memorable as the outward route. Retrace steps over the 'One Man's Pass' and walk east, the impressive corrie of Lough Agh down on the left, passing what is described as holy wells and an oratory. Drop to a narrow pass to their east and then climb the broad shoulder of Lergadaghtan Mountain (459m). From here continue south-east to meet, at a set of enclosures, the inland track up Slieve League, locally disparagingly called the 'Old Man's Track' (3.75 hours).

From here it is road, but a varied one, all the way to the start. Walk down from the enclosures, turn right at the tee, immediately cross a bridge and where instinct tells you almost infallibly to turn left downhill, turn right uphill. This track leads to the road on which you drove. Turn right onto it for the carpark. ■

ROUTE 34: SLIEVETOOEY

Slievetooey (511m), a 6km stretch of high ground rather than a single peak, faces northward over a mighty line of sea-cliff. This walk takes in part of the 6km stretch on the outward leg and returns on a difficult, undulating route high above the shore.

Getting There The start is about 6 miles west of Ardara. Take the N56 from the town towards Killybegs, turning right shortly at the sign 'Waterfall 6km' among others. Continue for about 5$\frac{1}{2}$ miles to park on waste ground in the hamlet of Maghera, where the road swings inland (GR 661906). **Buses** McGeehan's or Bus Eireann route 492 to near Ardara, though these are of limited value unless you can subsequently get a lift. **Bikes** can be hired in Ardara.

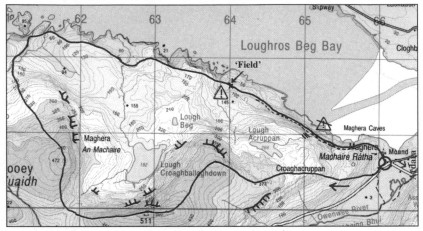

Walking Time 5.5 hours (distance 13km, climb 880m) including about 40 minutes extra after Gull Island for rough terrain and a narrow, hazardous path.

Difficulties There is rough, tiring ground for about 3km towards the end of the route. More important however is that you *must* find the path crossing the cliff face near Maghera. This path also involves a very mildly exposed few metres of scrambling. It is easier to find the path if you walk the route in the opposite direction to that given; the description given here should be adequate for either direction. However, this opposite direction means a difficult *descent* – more hazardous than an ascent – on the exposed section.

Now for the good news: navigation is generally easy and except as noted above, underfoot conditions good.

Map Sheet 10.

Route Walk onward from the parking place for a few hundred metres to about a track on the left and turn right here off the road to climb west towards the north-east spur of Slievetooey, crossing rough grazing ground and then sterner crags and outcrops. At length you will pass Lough Acruppan, which should be down on the right when you first see it. Continue onward to the bland mound (over 440m) terminating in far from bland cliffs on Slievetooey's north-east flank. Then swing south-west and shortly west over short grass and hags, keeping cliffs to the right to reach the trig pillar on Slievetooey (511m, 2 hours).

From this, the highest point on the route, Slieve League to the south-west and Crownarad to the south-east rise over vast expanses of bogland and low hill. The unmistakable sea stack of Tormore Island, shaped like the top of a child's crayon, and the Signal Tower near Sturrall are prominent features to the west, while to the north the headlands, peninsulas and islands of the west coast of Donegal stretch to the horizon.

Drop west to a narrow col, after which climb steadily northwards to reach pt 472m, an undistinguished top overlooking Lough Croaghballaghdown. From here head down a rocky slope roughly north-west, the idea being to reach a stream that reaches the sea just to the east of Gull Island. You may come across a few crags or even minor lines of cliff on this descent: if so veer right. When you reach the stream, cross it and follow a rough path to the cliffs close to Gull Island, a point of awe-inducing splendour where you can study the cliff-bound island continually pounded by the ocean (3.25 hours).

Curiously, the next section, the walk back to Maghera high above the sea, is far from the best section of cliff along this coast, mainly because the gentle upper slope conceals the full extent of sea-cliff below. There is a dilapidated fence and an intermittent path for much of the way, but the latter does not make the going much less tiring. Navigationally take care! From Gull Island you will pass three streams, the one you have already crossed and two others. The third stream is most important in order to find the path mentioned under 'Difficulties' above.

Just beyond this stream you will see what looks like a field with cuts along it. Walk across it (it's actually a small area of bog) and beyond it keep to about the same level, watching out for a path. Just beyond the bog you will cross an area of bracken that might conceal the path in summer and early autumn but you should be able to pick it up again after it. Once on it stick to it. It traverses the cliff face and as already indicated has one moderately bad step, reached a few minutes after crossing a small waterfall. Along here, by the way, the two peninsulas of Loughros Point and Dawros Head to the north are most impressive, should you have the nonchalance to study them.

Once close to the sand dunes, just keep heading east on paths wandering here and there until you reach a track leading to the starting point. Incidentally, if there is a low tide you might be interested in visiting the caves at the western end of the beach.

Longer Variation You can easily extend this route to pt 460m in GR 5990 and then walk north to majestic cliffs. The total walking time is 6.5 hours (distance 16km, climb 900m).

Inland Variation If you don't fancy the sea-cliff section of the main route, you can walk south-east from the trig pillar on Slievetooey to the high point on the road (at GR 6488) and then follow route 32 back. The total walking time is 4.25 hours (distance 12km, climb 620m). ■

ROUTE 35: GLENGESH

Though not the most exciting area in Donegal, the fine glacial valley of Glengesh, its long grassy slopes here and there steepening into formidable cliffs, is a good walking area (see the photo on OS map 10). You can do a simple circuit of the valley, but the route described here takes in a subsidiary valley and adds a touch of variety that that circuit lacks.

Getting There Take the N56 from Ardara towards Killybegs. After about $1^1/_2$ miles turn right off it (signed 'Glencolumkille 25km'). Continue for a short distance to park near the school on the right (GR 722888). **Buses** Bus Eireann table 298 bus or McGeehan's to the junction on the N56 in GR 7287, from where you can more conveniently start the walk. **Bikes** can be hired in Ardara

Walking Time 4.75 hours (distance 14km, climb 710m).

Difficulties Much soft and some very soft ground underfoot. Navigation moderately easy in an area where no hidden dangers lurk, though take care immediately after Common Mountain until you reach forest.

Map Sheet 10.

Route Walk back down the road from the school, turn right onto the N56 and right again, the only turn along here, after about 1km. Walk steeply uphill until what has become a track passes within a few metres of a stream on the left. Ford the stream here. (You have now paid the penalty - in the form of a road walk - for the slightly more complex circuit.)

Once across the stream climb roughly south-east to reach high ground. The first landmark is Lough Naweeloge, after which a fence will force you to swing right if the terrain doesn't. It's a steady and pleasant easy climb to Common Mountain (501m, 1.75 hours), which has a trig pillar and of course commands good long views.

The descent is not so pleasant as the ground gets gradually boggier as you advance. Head about south-west along the crest of the high ground and when, after 1.5km from the summit of Common Mountain, you reach the col facing Croaghnapeast, swing to north-west so as to keep a forestry plantation farther down on the right. Alongside the plantation the ground is really rough and rutted, so the road, when you hit it near its high point, will be welcome.

Cross the road and climb over boggy broken ground to Croaghavehy (372m), whose cairn lies at the far end of gently sloping ground, but is worth while reaching because of the good views it gives to the west. From Croaghavehy turn north-east to pass by the side of an upland plantation and then commence the climb through rocky buttresses forming the southern spur of Glengesh Hill. Along here you have excellent views of the cliffs that tower above the south-east side of Glengesh.

It may be no harm to seek out the summit of Glengesh Hill (385m) or, since it lies on gently sloping ground, at least its approximate location, as this will get you into line for the next stretch. (It has to be said that the following directions are far from being the only way to reach the valley floor and circumstances on the day may determine another approach.)

From the summit walk east steeply downhill. As you do so look out for two east running driveways, and aim just to the right of the longer, leftward one. Lower down you will find yourself in long, narrow upland fields running in the direction you are walking, a happy conjunction that minimises fence-crossing. You will pick up a path close to the driveway and this will allow you to pass by the associated house discreetly. Walk the driveway and at its end turn left for the nearby start. ■

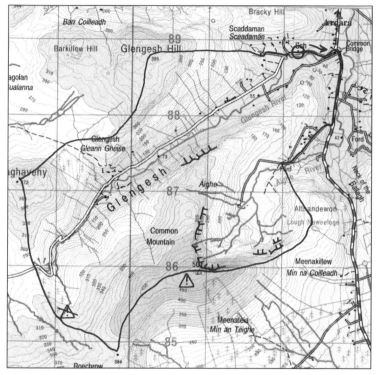

ROUTE 36: CROWNARAD

Crownarad (493m) is the highest point of a narrow south-running rocky ridge that briefly dominates the R263 west of Killybegs. To make a satisfactory circuit you will have to take a forest track along a narrow valley, but recent felling allows good views towards the ridge before you tackle it. The easy variation shortens this forest walk.

Getting There The start is about 7 miles west of Killybegs. Take the R263 from Killybegs towards Glencolumbkille, pass a prominent viewing point on the left, drive for a further 2.2 miles to take a narrow tarmac road on the right (there's a yield sign on the road which distinguishes it from the driveways around). Drive straight ahead for 0.6 miles and here fork left. You can park anywhere after this fork but for argument's sake let's say you park another 1.2 miles farther on where there is space off the track for a few cars (GR 660783). **Bus** Bus Eireann route 490 or McGeehan's, both of which run services along the R263.

Walking Time 4.5 hours (distance 14km, climb 580m).

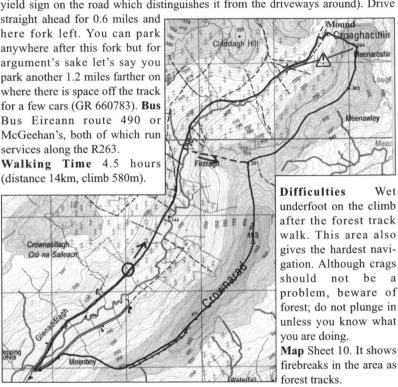

Difficulties Wet underfoot on the climb after the forest track walk. This area also gives the hardest navigation. Although crags should not be a problem, beware of forest; do not plunge in unless you know what you are doing.

Map Sheet 10. It shows firebreaks in the area as forest tracks.

Route Take the main track onward, that is the one running parallel to the line of the valley. Recent felling, you might be glad to hear, mitigates the monotonous sight of a million identical conifers. After about 15 minutes steady walking you will come to a gate and sheep pen set back on the right, the main stream in the valley beyond it, and a craggy hill beyond that again. If you are short of time or simply hate a forest trudge you should climb by this hill to reach the top of pt 381m, thus shortening the route by about one hour. (If the river is unfordable you can try crossing the elaborate bridge just upstream but at the time of writing felled trees block the way to the hill.

Otherwise, trudge on for about another 25 minutes, still keeping to the main track following the line of the valley. At this point you should cross a bridge with a narrow, low, concrete parapet on both sides. Seven minutes or so later, the track has just about levelled out and you will come to a distinct clearing on the right. If you walk a few metres into this clearing you will see on the left a wide, soggy firebreak. You can walk along this firebreak for about 100m to a mound with a really wide firebreak running off to the right (east). Otherwise you can take a small chance by walking along the track for the 100m to find the mound at a small gap in the forest. *Either way you must find this mound.*

A kind benefactor has cut lower branches of trees starting here, thus providing a direct path to unforested country. Hallelujah! From the mound, therefore, set your compass to 120° and follow the path. After a few minutes you will emerge from forest to reach the lower slopes of Croaghacullin (394m).

From Croaghacullin to the start of the climb to Crownarad over 2km away you are crossing rough bogland diversified by rock and outcrop. Simply keep to the indistinct crest of the ridge to climb pt 381 to the south-west, where the short variation rejoins the main route.

There is nothing much to distinguish pt 381m - like the minor summits before it, it hasn't even a cairn. Hopefully, however, you will recognise the col to its south, as it faces the formidable and unrelenting rise to Crownarad, beginning as a grassy slope broken by peat hags.

This climb to its northern summit (493m, 3 hours) is straightforward, the rocky ridge reaching its characteristically narrow aspect as you ascend. From the trig pillar marking the summit the views are excellent: Slieve League prominent to the west, an expanse of coastline and peninsula to the south and the escarpment of Benbulben across Donegal Bay. All of which and more to be enjoyed along the high ridge ahead.

The middle peak (over 460m) is topped by a high (perhaps 4m) metal spar, part of the wreckage from a British flying boat that crashed hereabouts in the Second World War. Continuing along the ridge the southern peak (471m) is reached after a short rise. Because it gives a view unimpeded by the main ridge this top probably offers the best panorama of all.

The descent requires a little initiative. Continue down the ridge for at least 1km, so walking parallel to a fence on the left. As you descend along the crest keep a watch rightwards for a suitable place to reach the road running along the south-east of the valley, but keeping in mind that it is easier to walk downhill along the crest rather than diagonally away from it. When I was last there I reached the road about 300m north-east of a prominent bridge carrying the other road in the valley (you will be able to see the bridge from the ridge). Whatever you do keep clear of sheep in fields and avoid proximity to houses.

On the road turn left, walk to the fork, turn right and walk to the start. Alas, the point where you started is clearly visible at the end of a road seemingly stretching almost to infinity ahead. Think about that pint you are going to enjoy! ■

ROUTE 37: GLENLOUGH AND THE ROSSAUN SEA CLIFFS

An adaptable route whose focus is what are probably the most impressive sea cliffs in Ireland – and that's saying something. There are several ways of getting to these cliffs and back again, of which this route, out over moorland and back a by minor road, is one. With the highest point, Slievetooey at only 460m, this is an ideal route for a day of low cloud.

Getting There From Ardara (GR 7390) take the N56 towards Killybegs, turning right off it after 1.3 miles, signed 'Glengesh Pass'. After another 3.8 miles turn right onto what looks like, from its width and condition, to be a road going nowhere. After another arduous 6.5 miles you will come to a signpost at a junction indicating directions for Port, Ardara and Glencolumbkille (GR 603886). Park considerately a few hundred metres beyond this junction.

From Glencolumbkille (GR 5384) drive to the police (garda) station and take the road signed Ardara. Fork left (signed Port) after 1 mile, continue straight ahead for 4.3 miles, turn left at the tee (it's the junction mentioned above) and park a few hundred metres along.

Walking Time 5.25 hours (distance about 15km, climb about 740m), approximations because it is difficult to judge distance and climb along the sea cliffs. In any case, you will probably want to linger along the cliffs.

Difficulties At first, a little attention to navigation required over rough terrain. After this the route is easy navigationally and underfoot.

Map Sheet 10.

Route Choose a place on the right (north) of the road where you can leave it without annoying locals or having to cross more than low fences (it's quite possible). As you do so, take a rough bearing aimed north at Slievetooey (460m), as its direction is not evident from here. This will take you initially over rough, boggy, undulating country and then, as you gain higher ground, into firmer terrain with a few outcrops. You will eventually find yourself above sizeable Lough Anaffrin on the left, fronted by a modest stretch of cliff and scree, and with only a short climb to the summit, which is cairned at its near end. From the summit continue north, keeping to the crest of a broad spur of dispiriting moorland, until you reach the sea cliffs.

From here on for the entire length of cliff there is nothing to the navigation: keep the sea on the right. Since you are no higher than 300m at any point, you can enjoy, even with low cloud, one of the finest stretches anywhere of sea cliff, pounding ocean, and rocky island. It's marvellous!

You will have to descend to nearly sea level at Glenlough, where the short variation heads for home (see below). For the main route you must walk a little upstream to cross the Glenlough River, which descends just before entering the sea in a series of waterfalls and pools between steep-sided banks, an area well worth exploring in detail.

Onward and upward. Ascend the seaward side of Port Hill, which ends abruptly at the great grass-topped block of Tormore Island, and then follow the coast generally downhill over springy grass to the tiny beach of sea-sculptured rocks at

Port. Port not only has a house, it also has a road: a veritable centre of urbanisation!

You are on road back all the way to the start, a straightforward walk of over 5km. This will take you initially through dull gently sloping country and then, around Killyfanned Lake, through more varied upland with the occasional homestead sheltering in the valley. A placid end to what should have been a memorable day.

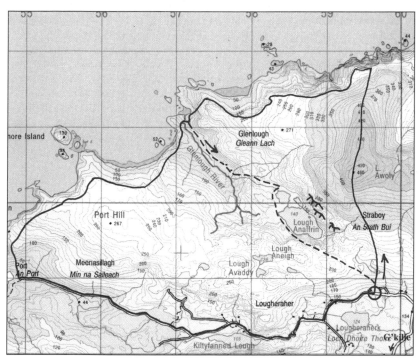

Short Variation You can easily come back from Glenlough. Follow the Glenlough River upstream, veering left from it to inspect two derelict houses built above the river. They were abandoned only in the 80's and much of the furniture and artefacts remain in one. From here a bearing initially east is needed to follow the correct stream to Lough Anaffrin. Keep the lake on the left and climb south-east from its shore to reach the road. Walking time from the estuary of the Glenlough River is 1.75 hours (distance 4km, climb 220m), allowing 15 minutes or so over Naismith for rough terrain. ■

ROUTE 38: TWO CLIFF WALKS BETWEEN GLENCOLUMBKILLE AND MAGHERA

The coastal stretch lying between Glencolumbkille at the far west of the Rossaun peninsula and Maghera (GR 6690) at its north-east corner, consists of magnificent ramparts of cliff, rocky off-shore island and inaccessible bay. I have chosen two walks, the first to give you a flavour of the area, the second a demanding but feasible expedition.

The Short Walk From Glencolumbkille (reached by Bus Eireann route 490 or McGeehan's) walk the main street, and with the church on the right, take the next turn right. Cross the bridge, turn first left and walk to the foot of steep ground to the north-west (yes, you can drive there if you are really lazy). Now simply walk along the top of the sea cliffs to the Signal Tower and beyond it to Sturrall, the rocky peninsula with a narrow, undulating crest projecting boldly oceanwards. Turn back at the base of Sturrall and take the same route back. You can slightly vary the return route by turning *left* onto the road at the foot of the high ground and taking it in a loop back to the village. The walking time is 2.75 hours (distance 10km, climb about 300m).

The Long Walk

Getting There Drive to Port (GR 5489), reached on a narrow but motorable road from the junction at GR 6088 (see route 37). This is an A to B route so a car will be needed at Maghera (see route 34).

Walking Time 6.5 hours (distance 17km, climb 1200m) but the climb can be reduced (see below).

Difficulties None, except on the seaward leg of route 34 should you choose it.

Map Sheet 11. The map extracts with routes 34 and 37 will give you most of the route.

Route Much of the route is described in routes 34 and 37 and it only remains here to give a summary and fill in the few gaps.

From Port climb the seaward shoulder of Port Hill and continue along the coast past Tormore Island to Glenlough (1.5 hours), recognisable by its deep-set river, where you will have to walk a little inland. Continue along the coast to Gull Island (route 34, 3.5 hours). Here you have a choice of the second part of route 34, which means a somewhat anti-climactic stretch of coast and a slightly perilous path and the first part of route 34 in reverse, which means wider views – and a stiff additional climb.

For variety I suggest that you go inland and upward, following the latter route in reverse, taking in pt 472m, which will certainly require a compass bearing from Gull Island. Then walk to the trig pillar on Slievetooey (511m), and so on following that route over Slievetooey's north-east spur (over 440m) back to Maghera. ■